John for Today

Reading the Fourth Gospel

Neil Richardson

scm press

© Neil Richardson 2010

Published in 2010 by SCM Press
Editorial office
13–17 Long Lane,
London, EC1A 9PN, UK

SCM Press is an imprint of Hymns Ancient and Modern Ltd
(a registered charity)
13A Hellesdon Park Road
Norwich NR6 5DR, UK

www.scm-canterburypress.co.uk

British Library Cataloguing in Publication data

A catalogue record for this book is available
from the British Library

978-0-334-04394-2

Originated by The Manila Typesetting Company
Printed and bound by
CPI Antony Rowe, Chippenham, SN14 6LH

Contents

Acknowledgements

I should like to thank Professors Morna Hooker and Judith Lieu of Cambridge University for their comments and suggestions on Chapters 1 and 3, respectively. And I should like to thank also members of my family – my wife, Rhiannon, and my sons Mark, James and Simon – for reading drafts of various chapters, and for helping me to make this book – as I hope it will be – accessible to all who are interested in exploring John's Gospel, one of the most influential Christian documents ever written.

Introduction: The Puzzle of John

This book is written for two groups of people: for those who find John's Gospel puzzling or difficult, and also for those who find it attractive and intriguing. I suspect that the first group greatly outnumbers the second. John's Gospel is a puzzle because it is so different from Matthew, Mark and Luke, which at least have a sort of family resemblance. Why is it different, and does it matter? Is John's Jesus just as much the real Jesus as the Jesus of the other Gospels? Does the fact of John's difference make this Gospel more – or less – reliable than the others?

It is a puzzle, too, because there is a 'Scarlet Pimpernel' quality about its author. The title so familiar to us, 'the Gospel according to John' probably reflects a Christian guess that the author was John, son of Zebedee. But was he? The evidence is intriguing, to say the least. Chapter 2 will address this question, as well as exploring the differences between John and the other Gospels.

In this book, however, I have taken the view that that is not the best place to begin. So we begin at the beginning by looking at the author's own prologue, his 'programme notes', which offer the reader an overview of the whole Gospel. The prologue also provides other perspectives on the Gospel – it is a story of a mission, a trial and of dramatic irony. Chapter 1 will explore these perspectives.

But John's Gospel is not only puzzling; it is, for many people, difficult. Its language is so stark and uncompromising: either/or, black and white, with no shades of grey in between. It strikes a discordant note in a world which prides itself on pluralism, or on a creed of relativism which invites people to say what is true for them and to reject the possibility of universal absolutes.

John's Gospel is difficult for modern readers in other ways. It sounds other-worldly, and seems to invite Christians to be other-worldly as well. In recent decades it has been much criticized for its alleged anti-Semitism, although 'anti-Jewishness' would be a better, less anachronistic term to use. Chapter 3 will seek to address these issues, together with the Gospel's apparent exclusiveness ('No one comes to the Father but by me', John 14.6), and the preponderance of male imagery when it speaks of God.

But in spite of its puzzles and difficulties, this Gospel presents a remarkably attractive message. Its leading themes, recurring again and again, are light and life. Most human beings who give the matter a moment's thought will recognize that there is something ambiguous, not fully realized, even distorted about human life; we are not as straightforward as other creatures. 'When is a human being really a human being?' is a question not often asked, and perhaps we are the poorer for it.

This Gospel insists that a world that neglects the divine gifts of light and life (for that is what they are) is courting destruction and death. Despite the failure of the world at large to see this, the most important issue it faces, according to John, is the truth and reality of God, the source of these gifts. In a century in which the world's penchant for self-destruction seems greater than ever, the message of John is urgently needed.

Chapter 4 fills out the details of these overviews, and takes us to the heart of John's message, giving due weight both to the historical foundations behind the Gospel, and to the theological 'commentary' which its author provides. Its four sections will guide the reader through the whole Gospel, focusing on the narrative's central figure, Jesus.

A final chapter, Chapter 5, explores the message of John for today. It focuses primarily on the question of God in a world of sometimes conflicting religions, and on 'the Christlike God' which this evangelist wants us to see. But there are searching implications in this Gospel for both the Church and the world at large, and this chapter will also examine these. This chapter, like earlier ones, will suggest that it is all too easy to misread this Gospel, to the impoverishment of the Church's witness and mission in the world. The Church, like the world at large, needs to hear afresh the message of this Gospel.

Many people know the Gospel's most famous verse: 'God so loved the world' (John 3.16). The wistful question of John Betjeman's Christmas poem comes to mind, 'And is it true? And is it true?' No one can prove or disprove it. But the wealth and profundity of John's Gospel, and – despite all the difficulties – its attractiveness, draw us to the quest. I hope this book will help many people on that journey.

I

Invitation to Life: The Story of a Mission

The prologue: author's guide to the story

If you go to see a play at the theatre, you may buy a programme in order to get a synopsis of the storyline. Of course, if the play was a 'whodunnit', you would hardly appreciate being told the identity of the murderer before the play had even begun. But it might be a play that you would understand better by getting beforehand an overview in the programme notes. John's Gospel begins with that kind of synopsis. So this is the obvious place for us to begin. As we shall see, John's prologue anticipates some of the Gospel's major themes, and we shall explore each of them in turn in subsequent sections of this chapter. We shall look, first, at the story of a mission; second, the drama and irony of a God present but unacknowledged in the world God made, and, last, the story of a conflict and trial, due to the world's rejection of the light. To begin with, however, we need to absorb the very informative programme notes which the author has put before us.

> In the beginning was the Word, and the Word was with God, and the Word was God. He was in the beginning with God. All things came into being through him, and without him not one thing came into being. What has come into being in him was life, and the life was the light of all people. The light shines in the darkness, and the darkness did not overcome it. (1.1–5)

When the evangelist writes the word 'God' (*theos*), to what, or to whom is he referring? A few years ago a church leader was questioned about the criticisms of 'god' made by the author of *The God Delusion,* Richard Dawkins. He responded that he, too, did not believe in the god criticized by Dawkins. In a similar way, we should not assume that what John's Gospel means by 'God' is what we mean. It may be that we are not clear what we mean. Christians can swing from embarrassed silence to chatter about God which is all too glib and easy ('poor talkative Christianity' was E. M. Forster's gibe). Perhaps, as my college chaplain once suggested, a moratorium on the word 'God' might do us all good. Alternatively, we can read with fresh eyes the Gospel of John, with its story of a 'Word', and the mission of that Word.

Many people hear the opening verses of the Gospel (1.1–18) at Christmas. But such is their depth and power, that even several hearings or readings do not exhaust their meaning. They start where the Bible itself starts: 'In the beginning'. But John[1] does not simply say, as the writer of Genesis does, 'In the beginning, God . . . ', but 'In the beginning was *the Word*'. That might suggest that there were two entities (for want of a better word) before creation: God *and* the Word. John seems to say two opposing things: 'the Word was with God, and the Word was God'. It is a mystery, like the mystery of 'the Father' and 'the Son' who will feature so prominently in what follows. They can be differentiated, like God and the Word, but, also like God and the Word, the Father and the Son are one (for example 10.30). So the Word is God, but not the whole of God. Does that mean the Word – and the Son – is a sort of lesser god?

In my student days, when my New Testament Greek was rather shaky, I had a doorstep conversation with a Jehovah's Witness. (It was a reversal of the usual roles, since I was the one on the doorstep.) He tried to persuade me that the Word was only *a* god, as distinct from Jehovah, who alone merited a capital 'G'. I subsequently learned that his Greek was worse than mine: the

---

1 It will be convenient to refer sometimes to the author of the Gospel as 'John'; on whether John was the author see Chapter 2.

evangelist says 'the Word was God' (that is the only God there is).² And in this eternal relationship between God and God's expression of himself in his 'Word', everything began.

But the opening verses say more: not only did all things have their origin through God and 'the Word', but what came into being was 'life', the kind of life which is the light of the human race (v. 4).³ Here the programme notes introduce us to two leading themes which will stay with us all the way through the story: light and life – the two go together. But there is darkness, too (v. 5). John does not tell us where it came from. But the good news is this: the light goes on shining in the darkness, and 'the darkness *did* not quench it', neither at the beginning when God began to make a world, nor even at the hour of a crucifixion, when the darkness was at its deepest.

> There was a man sent from God whose name was John. He came as a witness to testify to the light, so that all might believe through him. He himself was not the light, but he came to testify to the light. (vv. 6–8)

The scene changes – from heaven to earth. Enter the first witness: 'a man sent from God, whose name was John' (v. 6). He has only one task: 'to testify to the light' (v. 7). Our author is careful to say that John himself was not the light. In the opening scene of the drama, John himself will say as much (1.20), and again (3.28), when questioned by his own disciples. Perhaps there were people around who were saying he *was* the light; the Acts of the Apostles refers to 'disciples', perhaps disciples of John, who had been baptized by John, but had never heard of the Holy Spirit (Acts 19.1–7). So John the Baptist in this Gospel, more

---

2 The Witness argued that the Greek word *theos* doesn't have the definite article here, and so it must mean '*a* god' not '*the* God'. But since *theos* in John always refers to God, it must do so here. If John had put the definite article here, it would have meant that Jesus was, as it were, the whole of God: no first or third persons of the Trinity!

3 'Human race' translates the Greek word *anthropon*, a word that occurs with intriguing frequency in John.

even than in the other Gospels, acts in accordance with the in-
structions of a great conductor to his orchestra before a perfor-
mance of Beethoven: 'Gentlemen, I am nothing; you are nothing;
Beethoven is everything.'

> The true light, which enlightens everyone, was coming into
> the world. He was in the world, and the world came into be-
> ing through him; yet the world did not know him. He came
> to what was his own, and his own people did not accept him.
> (vv. 9–11)

From this spotlight on one man the focus widens – to the entire
kosmos (the Gospel's word for 'the world'). The world's existence is marked by a deep, tragic irony. It does not acknowledge
the light, utterly real and universal though that light is. The Creator (remember, 'the Word was God') was present in his own
creation, but unrecognized; in his own realm, but unwelcomed
by his own people (vv. 10–11). *When* was the Creator present?
What is John referring to here? His language, like poetry, is multidimensional: he could be referring to all history up to now (God
has always been present) or, more specifically, to the people of
Israel, since 'his own people' could equally refer just to them, as
well as to the whole world. But the writer may also mean the
very specific time when he came in 'the Word made flesh' – to
Israel and to the world. He probably wanted his readers to see
all three meanings in these words. But the fundamental point
stands: God was present, and people did not acknowledge him.

So there is only one true light, and its range is universal: 'it enlightens every human being' (v. 9). Is the light really universal, with
no human being left outside its illuminating power? That is what
our programme notes seem to say. This Gospel, as we shall see, is
remarkably inclusive: 'God so loved *the world*' (3.16), and 'when I
am lifted up from the earth, I will draw *all* people to myself' (12.32).
At the same time, there is a decision to be made, and universal
though the light is, people have preferred darkness to light (3.19).

So, in this synopsis we are reading before the drama itself begins, we could be listening to a commentary on the entire course

of human history. Or, we may be reading an outline of the drama our author is about to narrate. Or, such is his skill, we could be hearing both at once. But here is one of the distinctive features of John's Gospel: the whole world, the *kosmos*, is mentioned far more times than in any other New Testament book – more than in all of Paul's letters put together. This evangelist begins with the big picture, and never lets his audience forget it for long.

> But to all who received him, who believed in his name, he gave power to become children of God, who were born not of blood or of the will of the flesh or of the will of man, but of God. (vv. 12–13)

This fairly literal translation includes some difficult ideas.[4] The gift brought by the light may not at first seem very attractive to twenty-first-century people: 'to become children of God'. What that means will become clearer as the story unfolds. But no one can achieve that for themselves or for anyone else. Becoming a child *of God* has nothing to do with sex, with human desire, or (in a male-dominated world) what a man might want. Only God can make someone a child of God.

And that happens when someone 'believes in his name'. Here John is anticipating: 'his name' is the name of Jesus, but there is more to it than that. In almost the last occurrence of the word 'name' in John's Gospel, it becomes clear that Jesus all along has been entrusted with nothing less than the divine name: God has 'given' *his* name to his Son (17.11, compare 1.18 and 14.9) and, what is more, the Son did not keep it to himself: 'I made your name known to them, and will make it known' (17.26). The Gospel does not explicitly identify the name of Jesus with God's name, but it implies as much. In the Bible names are important, signifying not only identity, but character and, sometimes, power. (The name of the unregenerate Jacob, who cheated his brother Esau, meant 'supplanter' or 'deceiver' (Genesis 25.26);

---

4 Elsewhere in this book, unless otherwise stated, the translation used is the NRSV.

his new name was 'Israel', meaning, probably, 'the one who strives with God' (Genesis 32.28), and with this new name, Jacob, with a new penitence and humility, was reconciled to Esau (Genesis 33.1–16)). So God's name means God's power, God's character, God's very being. And all this Jesus has received and now reveals.

> And the Word became flesh and lived among us, and we have seen his glory, the glory as of a father's only son, full of grace and truth. (v. 14)

There is no verse quite like this anywhere else in the New Testament. Here is the fullest, clearest expression of what the Church was later to call 'the incarnation': God fully present in a human life. Other verses, such as Matthew's reference to 'Emmanuel . . . God is with us' (1.23), point in the same direction, but John 1.14 comes closest to the later doctrine. In his *Confessions* (7.9) the fourth-century theologian Augustine of Hippo compares the opening verses of John's Gospel with the writings of the disciples of the Greek philosopher, Plato. He tells us he found many of the same ideas in both the Gospel and the Platonists, though not in the same words. But he adds, 'that the Word was made flesh and dwelt among us, I did not read there'.

So 'the Word' – the very same Word which was with God at the beginning (v. 1) – took up residence 'among us' (v. 14), and in this human Word we saw the glory of a Father's one and only Son, full of undeserved love and unwavering faithfulness (literally, 'full of grace and truth', words central to God's character in the Old Testament – for example Exodus 34.6). And this love and faithfulness, this verse seems to say, *is* God's glory. It is a far cry from the glory of modern sport and the victories of modern warfare.

> John testified to him and cried out, 'This was he of whom I said, "He who comes after me ranks ahead of me because he was before me."' From his fulness we have all received, grace upon grace. (vv. 15–16).

We return to the witness of John the Baptist, a witness which, a present tense ('testifies') implies, continues into the present day (v. 15). Here John is quoting himself: 'He who comes after me . . .' (literally, 'behind me') is the same language used in the other Gospels of following Jesus. So a number of scholars incline to think that Jesus was a disciple of John before he embarked on his own independent mission. It is quite possible, and it is this Gospel, more than the other three, which seems to retain a memory of a certain 'rivalry' between John the Baptist and Jesus.

The Gospel's programme notes are so full, we can hardly do justice to them. But we mustn't miss another testimony that has crept in. Not only does John testify, but '*we*' do too: '*we* have seen' (v. 14). Whoever the author is – and we shall explore this question in the next chapter – he seems to be speaking for others, perhaps an entire Christian community. So, although it is useful to think of John's Gospel as a drama, it is not a drama of which we can be passive spectators. It is also the testimony of a whole community, telling us where life is to be found.

> From his fullness we have all received, grace upon grace. The law indeed was given through Moses; grace and truth came through Jesus Christ. No one has ever seen God. It is God the only Son, who is close to the Father's heart, who has made him known. (vv. 16–18)

So 'we' add our witness to John's (both the author's and the Baptist's): 'from his fullness we have all received grace upon grace' (v. 16). That sounds like an unstinting supply of grace, like the amount of wine which flows in a wedding at Cana (John 2.1–11). But the evangelist might just mean something else as well: 'grace *in place of* grace'. We easily contrast grace and law in our minds, associating grace with generosity and love, the law with sticking to the rules and, perhaps, being legalistic. So we tend to hear John as saying the law was given through Moses, *but* grace and truth came through Jesus. In fact, there is no 'but' in the original Greek. So 'grace in place of grace' may mean 'new' grace in place of the grace expressed in the law of Moses. 'The law *was given . . .*' was a Jewish way of saying '*God* gave the law'. So God's giving of the law through Moses was an act of grace; grace and truth in their fullness came through Jesus Christ.

This is the last time John will use the word 'grace', but it is the key to all that follows, and to all that has gone before. Grace and truth are the very heart of God's nature, as the Old Testament tells us. But now a fuller revelation has been given in the Word made flesh.

Finally, a truth which should be self-evident, but which religious people, including Christians, easily forget: 'no one has ever seen God' (v. 18a). That remains as true in the Christian era, as in the pre-Christian era. Yet there is probably no verb used as frequently by John as the word to see. All the way through his Gospel there is a tension between seeing and not seeing. People see, or think they see, but they don't really see (for example 9.41); people see, but need a deeper kind of seeing (for example John 6.26, 30) and, finally – and this is where the Gospel originally ended – some people have never seen Jesus as he was, yet may still come to faith (20.29).

That is the paradox on which the prologue ends: no one has ever seen God, yet 'it is God the only Son, who is close to the Father's heart, who has made him known' (v. 18).

So the curtain rises on a happening which defies definition, though some features of it are already becoming clear. The Gospel is the story of a mission. John the Baptist represents the advance party: the first emissary from God (v. 6), though this Gospel prefers not to think of him, as Mark and Matthew do, as Elijah (John 1.21, Mark 9.13, Matthew 17.12–13). The real language of mission, and especially 'sending' language, doesn't start properly until later in the story. But the prologue has 'trailed' it: light has come into the world. Was this really a mission? Yes it was, and it is, as a later verse will claim:

For God so loved the world that he gave his only Son, so that everyone who believes in him may not perish but have eternal life. (John 3.16)

But the Gospel of John is also a drama. Many of the people who first heard this Gospel read to them would have heard of – even if they had never visited – a theatre such as the one at Sepphoris, near Nazareth, or at Ephesus where, according to tradition, this Gospel was written. The Gospel is at times like a court-room drama: claims and counter-claims, charges and counter-charges will be made; where does the truth lie, and whom are we to believe? Testimony, rather than evidence, will be what matters.

Whether the evangelist borrowed this remarkable prologue from somewhere else, or borrowed and adapted it, or wrote it all himself, we cannot now know. Whether he wrote it when he began to write his Gospel or, more probably, after he had fin-ished it, we can't know either. (Preachers often realize the kind of introduction their sermon needs only when they've finished the sermon.) But our author has now set the scene, and in the next three sections of this chapter we shall fill out the outline of the story which his prologue has given us.

The story of a mission

People are sent on missions all the time. They always have been. People used to send their children to the local shop; in rural areas they still do. Salespeople are despatched the length and breadth of the country to sell their firm's products. An ambassador is sent to represent his country abroad. And mission statements – these days, it seems, two a penny! – attempt to say: 'We are here for a purpose, and this is what it is.'

A *father sent a son*

The society into which Jesus was born was less complex, but people were still sent on missions. In a Gospel parable a vine-yard owner sends first his servants and, finally, his son (for ex-ample Mark 12.1–11). It must have happened often. When a son learned his father's trade or helped on the farm, he would often undertake missions on his father's behalf.

So there was an everyday background to John's story of a mission: a father sent his son. That simple idea forms the basis of the most frequent way in which Jesus in this Gospel refers to God: 'the One who sent me', or 'the Father who sent me.' 'My food is to do the will of him who sent me . . . ' (4.34) is one of more than 40 expressions which refer to God sending Jesus. In this section we will sketch in outline John's story of the Son's mission.

The origin of the mission

John makes this very clear: it originates with God. Again and again in the Gospel the question is raised: *where is Jesus from?* People think they know when they don't (for example 7.27). Jesus himself knows where he is from (for example 8.14), but even at the end Pilate is raising the same crucial question: 'Where are you from?' (19.9).

People ask the same question about the gifts Jesus brings. 'Where do you get that living water?' asks the woman of Samaria (4.11). But no one, except Jesus, knows the origin of these gifts: 'the wind blows where it chooses, and you hear the sound of it, but you do not know where it comes from or where it goes' (3.8). The same theme crops up in the story of the first sign: the steward at the wedding tasted the water that had become wine, 'and did not know where it came from' (2.9, one of many hints that there is more to this story than first meets the eye).

Who authorizes any mission is quite crucial. The ambassador abroad represents his government back home. The business rep refers back to his line manager. In the first century, too, people were quite clear: a person who is sent (literally 'an apostle') 'is not greater than the one who sent him' (13.16). It was, and remains, one of the first principles of a mission, and 'the Son' was no exception: 'For I have not spoken on my own, but the Father who sent me has himself given me a commandment about what to say and what to speak' (12.49). Christians easily forget that Jesus was under orders. Curiously – or so it might seem – this appears not to detract from what the Church was later to call his divinity.

The mission's purpose and results

So much for the mission's origin. What of its purpose and effects? The work of Jesus is described in various ways in John: he takes away the sin of the world (1.29); glorifies God (for example 2.11; 13.32); he came to give life 'more abundantly'(10.10). But the purpose of his mission is stated most clearly of all quite early in the Gospel: 'Indeed, God did not send the Son into the world to condemn the world, but in order that the world might be saved through him' (3.17). The Gospel will say this again in Jesus' summary of his teaching (12.47). So John's Gospel accentuates the positive in a way that Christian evangelism and teaching often have not.

Yet this Gospel starkly portrays the dark background to God's mission to the world. It speaks of sin. These days that is an unfashionable word, but that doesn't mean it is a word which we can easily dispense with. What does sin mean in John? Not so much the moral failings, especially sexual ones, which we tend to associate with the word, but fundamentally a blindness to the origin and destiny of human life; namely the light and life which are the gifts of God. What God wishes to save the world from, according to John, are the self-destruction and death which result from turning our back on these gifts. It is perhaps worth adding – since it is so easy to read into the Bible words and ideas which are not there – there are no references in John to hell and eternal punishment. But the Gospel does speak of a judgement 'on the last day' (for example 12.48), and of the loss and destruction of which the world stands in danger (3.16).

There is yet another way of looking at the mission of the Son. Its purpose is not only to enlighten and to save the world, but also to glorify God. That is made very clear in the second half of the Gospel. The raising of Lazarus will reveal God's glory (11.4), as the miracle at Cana did (2.11). It is what Jesus prays for (12.28), the previous verse making clear that the hour of glory was why he came. But the Father who is the origin of the mission does not monopolize the glory (whatever this might be), like a director awarding himself a huge dividend, regardless of all the hard work done by the ones who actually carried out the mission. No, the glory of the Father and the Son are inseparable (13.31–32; 17.1). What this means we shall need to explore more fully. But revealing God's 'glory' will mean revealing God in his true colours, so to speak: God's true nature, beyond all the fantasies and distortions which we humans project on to God.

The progress of the mission

Did the mission go well, or did it fail? *Does* it go well, or is it failing? We might venture answers to these questions by simply looking around us: newspaper headlines, the strengths and weaknesses of local churches, and so on. We can't ignore these things, of course, but they would give us a very fragmented picture – or, perhaps, a skewed one. And how we read this contemporary evidence, if such it is, might depend on temperament: as the saying goes, the optimist sees a bottle half-full, the pessimist a bottle half-empty. But instead of simply looking around the world, we could look at this Gospel: its status as Scripture should encourage Christian readers to believe that it will be a reliable guide today in helping us to understand how God's mission goes in the world.

The prologue flags up three things about that mission. It meets with ignorance and opposition: 'he was in the world, and . . . the world did not know him'; he came to what was his own, and his own people did not accept him (1.10–11). But it also meets with some success: 'to all who received him . . . From his fullness we have all received . . .' (1.12, 16). Is that success or failure? The question remains open. But of one thing we can be sure – and this is the third point – 'the light goes on shining . . . and the darkness has never overcome it' (1.5).

The opening chapters of the Gospel fill out this summary of acceptance and opposition. Disciples respond to the call of Jesus (1.35–51); they see his glory in the first sign at Cana and believe (2.11), and many Samaritans, too, come to faith (4.39). Nicodemus, however, remains in the dark (3.2). As for the level of opposition, the Old Testament text which the evangelist includes in his version of the cleansing of the Temple anticipates a level of opposition which will prove lethal: 'zeal for your house will consume me' (2.17). The comments which follow Jesus' conversation with Nicodemus also strike a bleak note, especially the observation that 'people loved darkness rather than light' (3.19). (The NRSV puts them in quotation marks, but it is difficult to be sure where, in this chapter, the words which the evangelist attributes to Jesus actually end.[5])

The chapters that follow tell us again and again that Jesus' opponents wish to do away with him (5.18; 7.1; 7.25; 8.37, 40). Plans to arrest Jesus are thwarted (7.30, 32, 44) not only because the opposition is divided, though some are impressed in spite of themselves (7.45–47), but because of an overarching providence, it would seem, ensuring that Jesus will not be arrested until his 'hour' has come (7.30; 8.20), the very point Jesus made back in Cana (2.4).

Subsequent chapters reveal a twofold development in the unfolding of God's mission to the world. A new community is beginning to emerge: Martha, Mary, and Lazarus raised from the dead (chapter 11) are among its first representatives. Meanwhile, the opposition does not diminish. Jesus narrowly avoids a lynching (10.31) and another attempt to arrest him (10.39). Some are not persuaded even by the raising of Lazarus, Jesus' last and greatest sign. Instead, it hastens a plot to kill Jesus (11.46–53). There is a sense of Jesus biding his time (11.54). But at last the king comes to his own realm (12.12–15), even though it is in Jerusalem that his enemies await him (11.57).

There is an air of finality about the last verses of chapter 12. The verse from Isaiah (Isaiah. 6.10) used by the other evangelists of the tragic rejection by God's people of God's Messiah is used here by John: 'He has blinded their eyes and hardened their heart . . .' (12.40).

---

5 There are no quotation marks in our Greek manuscripts of the New Testament, and so sometimes a translator simply has to try to work out where direct speech ends.

The climax of the mission

So this phase of the mission comes to a close. The Son has borne his witness, stated his credentials, and fulfilled the task his Father gave him by offering his gifts of life and light, of bread and wine. Now the mission moves to its climax: the hour has come (12.23; 13.1; 17.1). The opposition will do its worst, and *at the same time*, the glory of God will be revealed, the glory of the Father and the Son.

So we come back to one of the basic principles of any mission, then and now: the one who sends is greater than the one who is sent (for example 14.28). Jesus comes from God, and goes back to God. In this mission, what the Father has entrusted to his Son is quite simply 'everything' (3.35; 5.20; 13.3). And here there is no mistaking the triumphant note in Jesus' final words from the cross, 'It is finished' (19.30): mission accomplished.

That, of course, is to express it too baldly. The state of the world gives us pause, to say the least. Yet John's Gospel is quite clear: the Son has accomplished the mission entrusted to him by the Father (17.4; 19.30). What had Jesus done? There are as many answers to that question as there are to the question, 'what was the purpose of the mission?' Jesus has revealed the divine glory: some, at least, have come to see what before they had not seen. He has shared his gifts and, in the process, created a new community under 'one shepherd' (10.16). That was no easy task. The new community had to be 'kept' and 'guarded'(17.12), hated and persecuted as they were in a dark, unbelieving world.

The mission goes on

There is one more thing to add. One of the principles governing missions in the world of Jesus was this: an agent can appoint another agent; one sent on a mission may, in turn, send others in furtherance of that same mission. That is what Jesus, as the Father's agent, does: 'As the Father has sent me, so I send you' (20.23).

To return to the prologue: the story of a Son sent by his Father is the story of the Word which was with God 'in the beginning'.

The aim of the mission is what the prologue says it was – and is: to bring light and life to the world. Light and life, according to this Gospel, go together, and the source of both is God.

A story of dramatic irony

The prologue sets the scene for looking at the Gospel of John in another way: it is a drama. This doesn't mean that it is fiction; in the view of the author and of the Christian Church, this drama is true. But in many ways it is presented in dramatic form, and that should not surprise us; the writer is serious about getting his message across.

John's Gospel as a drama

I suggested earlier that most of the Gospel's first readers (or hearers) would be familiar enough with drama. This would have been even more likely if the Gospel was completed at Ephesus, where the ruins of the theatre can still be seen today. So it is possible that the world of Greek drama was on the writer's own doorstep. But before we look at dramatic features of the Gospel – and one characteristic in particular – consider the privileged perspective which the prologue has given you, the reader. This is not a thriller, where it would be vital that the audience is *not* told the whole story. This is more like a classic; we know the story, but because it says something profoundly true about life, about human beings and – in this case – about God, it has a power all its own. With writing like that, a prologue can give the drama which follows even greater power and poignancy.

The prologue starts in heaven and moves to earth: 'in the beginning was the Word . . . and the Word became flesh'. So it gives us, first, a view from heaven, and an overview of the whole story. That means that you, the reader, will know more than any of the characters in the story, except Jesus himself.

What are the Gospel's dramatic features? First, and most obvious, there is a lot of conversation, almost entirely between Jesus and others: the disciples, 'the Jews', Nicodemus and the Samaritan woman are prime examples from the first four chapters. In chapters 5—8 Jesus' conversations – increasingly acrimonious – are mostly with 'the Jews' (on this see Chapter 3 below). Chapters 9 and 11 comprise two of the most dramatic passages of all: the healing of the blind man and its consequences (9.1–44), and the raising of Lazarus, and its aftermath (11.1–53). Act 1 of John's drama moves to its climax in chapter 12, as we saw in the last section, as Jesus announces (12.28) that his hour has come, and recapitulates the main themes of his public teaching (12.44–50).

Act 2 opens dramatically enough with the story of Jesus washing his disciples' feet (13.1–16). The tragedy of Judas is powerfully portrayed (vv. 18–30), culminating in, 'So, after receiving the bread, he went out. And it was night' (v. 30). Thereafter, there is a distinct change of mood, with the farewell discourse of Jesus to his disciples (chapters 14—16), followed by his prayer to the Father (chapter 17). The readers and audiences of John's world would be familiar enough with the genre of a farewell discourse, especially if they knew the Jewish Scriptures, as many of them would. A farewell discourse, such as those of Jacob, Joseph and Moses in the Old Testament and Paul in the New (Acts 20.17–35), consisted of words of wisdom imparted by a leader prior to his death in order to give guidance to his followers when he was no longer with them. Such is the final discourse of Jesus in this Gospel.

But in the dramatic flow of John's Gospel, they serve another purpose. Together with chapter 13 these chapters explain in advance what the evangelist will narrate in the remaining chapters of the Gospel (18—20). So while the last three chapters narrate the external events (though they do far more than that), the earlier ones alert the reader to their deeper significance.

To see or not to see?

Although the long discourses of Jesus dominate some sections of this Gospel, we mustn't miss the dramatic style and content of the rest of the Gospel – particularly its many conversations. But there is a second dramatic feature of this Gospel that would 'ring bells' with its first audiences. Many a drama in John's world hinged on stories of recognition and non-recognition. It was a familiar theme. In Homer's *Odyssey* Odysseus returned from his travels incognito. In Euripedes' tragedy *The Bacchae* Agave tragically failed to recognize her own son Pentheus and, most famous of all, in Sophocles' *Oedipus Rex* Oedipus did not know that he had killed his own father and taken as his queen his own mother Jocaste.

This brings us to a recurring feature of the Gospel, already outlined in the prologue: dramatic irony. There are many examples of irony, but they all hinge on one thing: the identity of Jesus, and on whether other characters recognize him for who he is:

> He was in the world, and the world came into being through him; yet the world did not know him. He came to what was his own, and his own people did not accept him. (1.10–11)

Dramatic irony in John takes two forms. First, people are portrayed time and again as knowing less than they think. They imagine they know who Jesus is – but they don't. Such characters prompt from us, the audience, the response, 'That's what they think!', or 'How wrong can they be!' But we have had the privilege of hearing the prologue.

As we might imagine, the origins of Jesus are the cause of much irony. 'Can anything good come out of Nazareth?' asks Nathaniel (1.46). 'Rabbi,' says Nicodemus (this very way of addressing Jesus shows how much Nicodemus has yet to learn), 'we know that you are a teacher come from God' (3.2). To this the audience mutters something like, 'That's the understatement of the year!'

And so it goes on. 'Are you greater than our father Jacob?' asks the Samaritan woman (4.12) – the irony of saying this to the Son of God! 'Are you greater than our father Abraham?' ask the Jews (8.53). The irony of these two questions is especially sharp in the original Greek, which shows that the questioners expect the answer 'No – surely not!'

There is a particularly interesting example of irony in chapter 6. The Jews ask, 'Is not this Jesus, the son of Joseph . . .?' (6.42). This

time the question expects the answer, 'Yes – of course you are!' We
don't know whether the writer of the Gospel knew of the tradition
of Jesus' virginal conception, referred to in the Gospels of Matthew
and Luke, but whether he did or not, this question is still misplaced,
because Jesus is *God's* Son, and that is the only origin that matters.
So here is another example of characters in John's drama thinking
they know when they don't. There is another example, when the
people in Jerusalem say 'we know where this man [that is Jesus]
is from; but when the Messiah comes, no one will know where he
is from' (7.27). This is one kind of dramatic irony: characters in
John's drama think they know when they don't.

The irony sometimes takes a different form. Whereas some
people know less than they think, others say more than they
realize. But, again, all the examples focus on the identity of
Jesus. The words of the wedding steward at Cana may be an early
example: 'you have kept the good wine until now' (2.10).

There is a variation on this pattern of people saying more than
they realize. Sometimes their words, unbeknown to them, are
prophetic: their words have come true in a way that they, portrayed as contemporaries of Jesus, could not have foreseen. So
the Jews ask, 'Does he intend to go . . . and teach the Greeks?'
(7.35). By the time this Gospel was completed, the disciples of
Jesus had taught many Greeks (compare 12.19). But perhaps the
most poignant example of this kind of irony comes in the words
of Caiaphas towards the end of Act 2: 'You do not understand
that it is better for you to have one man die for the people than
to have the whole nation destroyed' (11.50). 'One man die for
the people': Caiaphas said more than he knew. In fact, this is one
example of irony that was important enough for the evangelist
to explain in the verse which follows (v. 51).

The fundamental irony

It would be a mistake to think that these examples of irony merely
demonstrate how clever the author of the Gospel was. Behind
and beneath all the irony is the fundamental irony: the Creator
of the world has come to his world, and his world cannot, or

will not, recognize him. So the evangelist's irony is a vehicle of truth.

So people can be mistaken – profoundly mistaken – about their true condition. It happens all the time: a nation may pride itself on its democracy and its prosperity, and yet be morally and spiritually impoverished; a church may think it is doing very well, when the opposite is true. John 9 is an extended example of this kind of irony. A man born blind, who might therefore be thought to be a sinner, born of sinners (vv. 1–2) and whom people still dismiss as a sinner even after Jesus has given him his sight (vv. 30–34), is portrayed here as a model disciple, rather like another blind person healed by Jesus – Bartimaeus in Mark 10.45–51. But whereas Mark only hints at the discipleship of Bartimaeus ('he . . . followed him in the Way' (Mark 10.51)), the physical healing of the blind man in John's Gospel is only the beginning of his transformation. Like many subsequent Christian disciples, the controversy he becomes embroiled in only serves to deepen his understanding of Jesus. Questioned by neighbours and others, all he can say at first is that 'the man Jesus' healed him (v. 11). Soon he is telling the Pharisees, 'He is a prophet' (v. 17). At a second interrogation, he is bolder still: he gives the Pharisees a veritable lecture, culminating in, 'If this man were not from God he could do nothing' (v. 33). Finally, on his expulsion (presumably from the synagogue (vv. 34–35), Jesus sought him out, and invited him to believe in himself as the Son of Man, and the man's initiation as a disciple of Jesus is complete: 'He said "Lord, I believe". And he worshipped him' (v. 38).

By contrast, the Pharisees think they know (v. 16), when they do not (compare v. 24). Confident in their false knowledge, they are happy to be ignorant of the most important question of all; dismissively they say of Jesus, 'as for this man, we do not know where he comes from' (v. 29b). This story, with the ironical contrast between the once-blind man and the Pharisees, ends with a succinct summary of the irony which has run throughout:

Jesus said, 'I came into this world for judgement so that those who do not see may see, and those who do see may become

blind'. Some of the Pharisees near him heard this and said to
him, 'Surely we are not blind, are we?' Jesus said to them, 'If
you were blind, you would not have sin. But now that you say,
"We see", your sin remains.' (vv. 39–41)

The irony of John's Gospel comes to its climax in the story of the
trial of Jesus before the high priest (18.19–24), and then Pontius
Pilate (18.28—19.16). We, the readers, know what is really going on, because we have been told. Jesus is the one who appears
to be on trial as the authorities interrogate him. In fact, something quite different is happening: 'Now is the judgement of this
world' (12.31). I once read that a man looking round the Na-
tional Gallery in London informed an attendant that he didn't
think much to the pictures on display. The attendant replied, 'It
is not the pictures, sir, which are on trial.'

The gift of revelation

Two themes emerge from our brief overview of John's irony,
centred as it is on the identity, and therefore the recognition or
non-recognition, of Jesus. First, how do people in this Gospel
recognize Jesus? It was clearly not a matter of being clever, or
more perceptive than, say, the Pharisees. True revelation was –
and is – more mysterious than that. It is always a gift. So the
Samaritan woman eventually acknowledges – perhaps, rather
than 'recognizes' – Jesus as the Messiah whom her people are ex-
pecting because Jesus tells her 'I am he' (4.26); the royal official
comes to faith through the healing of his son (4.46–54); both the
blind man, as we have seen (9.35–37), and Martha (11.25–27)
come to faith because of Jesus' self-declaration to them.

So this all-important revelation is a gift, rather than a puzzle
which people work out for themselves. No one can take any
credit for becoming a disciple. In fact, Jesus says as much: no one
can come to God (or Jesus) unless the Father 'draws' them (6.44,
65); 'you did not choose me, I chose you' (15.16a). This is difficult for us to understand in consumer societies intoxicated with
choice. The best analogy in human experience to this mysterious

gift from God is falling in love, or 'clicking' with someone who becomes a firm friend for life. There is still a commitment to be made. But we don't simply choose these wonderful experiences – they just happen.

Responsibility for unbelief

Second, however, John's Gospel makes it clear that people are responsible for their own unbelief. The words which conclude Jesus' discussion with Nicodemus seem to say it is all a matter of whether people prefer darkness to light (3.19–20). Of course, the reasons why people believe or do not believe are usually varied and complex. Some people born into an enlightened Christian home may move seamlessly into faith. Others, born into a repressive 'Christian' home, may be put off for life.

So we are faced, it seems, with a deeply unfair situation: we can't make ourselves believe, any more than we can fall in love; only God can bring us to faith. Yet, according to John, we are responsible for our unbelief, even though there may be all kinds of reasons for it. It helps, I think, to keep recalling the fundamental human need for love – from the moment we are born. As I have said, we can only be (eventually) grateful recipients of parental love, if we have been so fortunate; like falling in love, we could hardly have arranged it for ourselves. Encountering Jesus, this Gospel seems to say, is that kind of experience: finding a friend for life. It also helps, I find, to remember that although some verses in the New Testament seem to suggest otherwise, God is not a 'choosy' God, selecting some in unfair or arbitrary preference over others. God loves all (John 3.16; see also 1 Timothy 2.4, which insists God wants everyone 'to be saved').

The climax – and paradox – of the revelation

As with the irony of John's 'drama', the theme of recognition and non-recognition comes to its climax in the crucifixion and resurrection of Jesus. The evangelist had flagged this up in some earlier words of Jesus: 'When you have lifted up the Son of Man, then you will realize that I am he' (8.28). Did these words really come true? How extraordinary, that anyone should recognize Jesus in the hour of his greatest agony and humiliation! But John doesn't emphasize the undoubted historical realities of a crucifixion. He sees it differently. 'The hour' of Jesus, as the evangelist calls it (2.4 onwards), is the hour of the divine paradox. The translation 'lift up' conveys something of the ambiguity of the Greek and, so many scholars think, the Aramaic which may lie behind the Greek. Jesus will indeed be 'lifted up' when the cross is hoisted into place. But *that* will be the hour of his glory. It's as if, through long reflection on the inscription above the cross, 'the king of the Jews', this evangelist had come to see that the cross was indeed the enthronement of Jesus, and therefore the revelation of the divine glory.

So is the crucifixion the supreme example of God incognito? It would seem so: 'He was in the world . . . yet the world did not know him' (1.10). That is the supreme – and tragic – irony. But the evangelist sees something else going on. Even as Jesus hangs on his cross, he ensures that his mother adopts a son and that son his mother – the creation of a new community (19.26–27). (On this passage, see also Chapter 2 below.) Most remarkable of all, against all outward appearances, a victory has been won: Jesus' final words tell of something accomplished: 'It is finished' (v. 30). Nor is that all. In the very next verse a double entendre in the original Greek might mean, not only that Jesus 'gave up his spirit', but also that, in fulfilment of his promise to his disciples, 'he . . . handed over the Spirit' (v. 31).[6]

Almost from start to finish, there is dramatic irony in John's Gospel. It comes to a climax in the trial and death of Jesus: he came to his own, and his own did not receive him – him, the Creator of the world. This is the truth – and the challenge – at the heart of the world: God offers his gifts of life, light and love. Will

---

6 Two facts suggest that this verse is one with a double meaning: the word 'his' is not there in the Greek and, second, in our oldest manuscripts all letters are capital letters ('uncials'), so it is not clear whether John meant 'spirit' or 'Spirit'. It is likely that he meant both.

the world respond or not? That question brings us to the third of our perspectives on this Gospel, arising from the prologue.

The story of a trial

There is one more overview of the Gospel anticipated by the author's programme notes in chapter 1.1–18. To judge from the reference to John the Baptist in verse 6, testimony will play an important part in the unfolding drama of the mission of 'the Son', and John's Gospel is full of what we might call 'courtroom' language. But we need to distinguish between a modern court of law, and what would have been the practice in the time of Jesus.

Imagine a Palestinian village or town and a public space where two ways meet. There is a small gathering of five or six men. One man is accusing another of telling malicious lies about him. The other man is the accused; he hotly denies the charge, and he has a friend to support him. The other men are the village or town elders, who will try to decide who is telling the truth. This was the informal ad hoc court. In such a trial, the role of witnesses will be crucial. Did they see or hear the alleged lies? And are these witnesses reliable? ('Only on the evidence of two or three witnesses shall a charge be sustained' (Deuteronomy 19.15; 2 Corinthians 13.1)).[7]

Witnesses

The first example of 'courtroom' language occurs in the prologue itself: enter the first witness to Jesus, in the person of John the Baptist (1.6). He has no role other than that of simply witnessing to the one who, though he came after John, was well and truly 'first' (v. 15). But John is only the first in a long line of witnesses. He might be said to summarize the Scriptures (5.39), which, this

---

7 One of the principal ways in which the author urges his case is simply by repeating himself. This was the way in which a Jewish contemporary would have attempted to win the argument in a legal dispute.

Gospel tells us, contain other witnesses to Jesus: Moses (5.46), Abraham (8.56), and Isaiah (12.41).

Many others 'line up', as it were, in John's story, to testify to Jesus. The first disciples, including a 'true Israelite' in the person of Nathaniel (1.46–49), bear witness to a gradually unfolding revelation. Others do likewise: the Samaritans acknowledge 'the Saviour of the world' – a striking riposte, perhaps, to Roman imperial pretensions. Simon Peter, in what may be this Gospel's equivalent of his confession at Caesarea Philippi in Mark (Mark 8.29), declares, 'We have come to believe and know that you are the Holy One of God' (6.69).

But there are others in John's story with a less favourable testimony. The crowd accuses Jesus of being possessed (literally of 'having a demon', 7.20); 'the Jews' follow suit (8.48, 52; 10.20), later accusing him of blasphemy (10.33), and the Pharisees tell the once-blind man that Jesus is a sinner (9.24).

'Signs'

There is more 'courtroom' language in what this Gospel says about 'signs'. This particular word had a history. It occurs in the Old Testament story of the Exodus: Moses presented one sign after another to Pharaoh, but 'Pharaoh's heart was hardened' (for example, Exodus 4.21; 7.3). In John's story, as we have seen, the turning of water into wine is the first sign (2.11), the healing of the royal official's son the second (4.54). The evangelist doesn't continue his numbering of Jesus' miracles, but there are seven in all, eight, if we count the resurrection: the healing of the crippled man (5.1–9), the feeding of the five thousand (6.1–15), Jesus walking on water (6.16–21), his healing of the blind man (9.1–7), and the raising of Lazarus (11.1–44).

The argument about the 'signs' Jesus gave are part of the argument 'in court'. The signs were proof, or otherwise, that this person was telling the truth. So there is an ongoing debate. As in the other Gospels, people ask for a sign (2.18; 6.30); others, like Nicodemus, argue that Jesus could not do these signs unless God were with him (3.2, compare 9.16).

As the story unfolds, the question is no longer *whether* Jesus performed signs, but how many (7.31), and what it all adds up to (7.31; 11.47). Opinion was divided even among those who saw what Jesus did, whether it was miraculously feeding a crowd, or raising Lazarus from the dead. What mattered was how they read 'the sign', or, rather, whether they realized that what had happened was a sign pointing beyond itself to the truth behind it. Were they simply spectators – satisfied customers (6.26)? Or did they see where, or to whom, the sign was pointing?

So the signs are evidence adduced in the trial which is taking place. Yet they are not proofs. The purpose of the evangelist in recounting them, as we have seen, was to lead people to faith (20.30–31), but the first part of the Gospel ends on a downbeat note: 'Although he had performed so many signs in their presence, they did not believe in him' (12.37).

The summing up

Shortly after this sad observation, Jesus concludes with what might be called a summing up in the trial. As we noted in the previous section, these verses are an important recapitulation of the whole of John's Gospel so far:

> Then Jesus cried aloud: 'Whoever believes in me believes not in me but in him who sent me. And whoever sees me sees him who sent me. I have come as light into the world, so that everyone who believes in me should not remain in the darkness. I do not judge anyone who hears my words and does not keep them, for I came not to judge the world, but to save the world. The one who rejects me and does not receive my word has a judge; on that last day the word that I have spoken will serve as a judge, for I have not spoken on my own, but the Father who sent me has himself given me a commandment about what to say and what to speak. And I know that his commandment is eternal life. What I speak, therefore, I speak just as the Father told me.' (12.44–50)

So the trial reaches its climax. Ostensibly, it was the trial of Jesus; in fact, it is the world's, even though Caiaphas, Pilate and other representatives of 'the world' cannot see that. In this trial, the reader is left in no doubt about the most fundamental issue of all: is Jesus from God, or isn't he? Is he speaking the truth in claiming that God sent him, and that God is his Father, and he is God's Son? As we have seen, witness after witness testifies, beginning with John the Baptist and ending with the disciple whom Jesus loved. Scripture itself, and three of its leading figures, testify on Jesus' behalf. But there are three more witnesses, beginning with Jesus himself.

The witness of the Son, the Father and the Spirit

Was a man allowed to testify on his own behalf? Yes, he was. But his testimony wasn't necessarily accepted. One crucial question was: did he know what he was talking about? Had he seen and heard for himself what he was claiming to have seen and heard? This Gospel insists Jesus had (8.26).

But, besides Jesus himself, there is another witness. What a defendant did was to invoke God as his witness. On three occasions – when he was seeking to counter serious criticism of himself – Paul did so (2 Corinthians 1.23; 11.31; Galatians 1.20). But to invoke God as your witness was, to put it somewhat crudely, to play for high stakes. If you called in God on your side, and you weren't telling the truth then, it was widely believed, you were asking for serious trouble; you were risking divine punishment.

In the view of this Gospel, God himself was Jesus' most important witness. Jesus' witness, by itself, would not be true but, underwriting all that Jesus said and did, was the Father. This is why the evangelist allows Jesus, as it were, to contradict himself (compare 8.13–14 with 5.31): Father and Son are 'hand in glove': their testimony is one and the same.

There is one more witness. This witness, the Holy Spirit, brings us down to the present day. One of this Gospel's distinctive words for the Holy Spirit is 'the Advocate' (the Greek is *paracletos* – for example 15.26). Here is more courtroom language: an advocate was someone enlisted as a special friend (as in our imaginary example), to testify on the defendant's behalf, refuting the charges. But if the charges were proven to be unfounded, then the tables were turned, and that friend became a sort of counsel for the prosecution against those who had brought the charges. This is exactly what the farewell discourse (John 14—16) says about the Holy Spirit: the Spirit of truth testifies to Jesus, and stands by the disciples, but convicts the world: 'When the Advocate comes . . . the Spirit of truth who comes from the Father, he will testify on my behalf. You also are to testify . . .' (15.26–27). At the same time, 'when he [that is the Advocate] comes, he will prove the world wrong' (16.8).

For or against?

This is one of the most difficult features of John's Gospel: its black and white character. In this respect it reflects or develops what Jesus says in Mark's Gospel: 'Whoever is not against us is for us' (Mark 9.40, compare Luke 9.50). But it is important not to misunderstand or misuse this theme. It is an oversimplification to say that Jesus was mad, bad or God. But there is no doubt that John's Gospel makes more explicit what underlay the other Gospels: either Jesus was speaking the truth in what he said about God, or he was not. No one could sensibly say that Jesus was half-right, or that God was with him some of the time, but not all the time. It was all or nothing.

Curiously, in the trial of Jesus in Jerusalem, the charges against him are not as explicitly stated as in the other Gospels, where he is variously accused of saying that he would (Mark 14.58) or could (Matthew 26.61) destroy the Temple, and of subverting the nation and stirring up the people (Luke 23.2, 5). There is another surprise here. In the other Gospels the question of Jesus' identity is central to his trial though Matthew, Mark and Luke differ in what they record Jesus as saying (Mark 14.61–62; Matthew 26.63–64; Luke 22.66–70). But in John's account the only reported interrogation centres on the disciples of Jesus and his teaching (v. 19). It is only as Pilate insists on Jesus' innocence that John has 'the Jews' say, 'We have a law, and according to that law he ought to die because he claimed to be the Son of God' (19.7).

This story of a trial seems a bleak, even forbidding one, speaking as it does of the world's preference for darkness, rather than light, and of the judgement consequent upon that. But twice the Gospel insists: Jesus did not come to judge the world (3.17; 12.47). That was not his purpose. Yet the coming of the light into the realm of darkness inevitably resulted in exposing the darkness for what it was. The symbol of light, as always in John, stands for reality: the reality of God, and the life-giving truth which God gives. So, paradoxical though it may sound, God's love is the origin of the judgement. That is contrary to God's intention, but 'unbelief, by shutting the door on God's love, turns his love into judgement. For this is the meaning of judgement, that man shuts himself off from God's love.'[8]

And a conclusion

Just as this Gospel has a clearly demarcated prologue, it also has a clear-cut conclusion, and a clear statement of why the author wrote the Gospel (20.30–31):

> Now Jesus did many other signs in the presence of his disciples, which are not written in this book. But these are written so that you may come to believe that Jesus is the Messiah, the Son of God, and that through believing you may have life in his name.

The evangelist ends where he began: talking about *life*. This Gospel illustrates what Bishop John V. Taylor wrote: God is not so much interested in making us religious, as in making us alive. (It provides a striking contrast with the frequently heard remark, 'I'm not really religious'.)

---

8 R. Bultmann, *The Gospel of John. A Commentary*, Oxford: B. Blackwell, 1971, p. 154.

31

John is very clear about the source of life: Jesus Christ. It is far from obvious to most people today, especially in a world of many faiths. We shall need to explore what this striking claim means. We 'access' life, according to the Gospel's conclusion through 'believing' – again, easier said than done. For now, we simply note John's distinctive voice: he uses the word 'believe' more times than Matthew, Mark and Luke put together and, in contrast to Paul, who uses the word 'faith' far more often than 'believe', John never uses the word 'faith' at all. (In Greek 'faith' *pistis* and 'believe' *pisteuo* come from the same root.⁹)

We easily stumble these days over the words 'belief' and 'believing'. They are associated with the Church's 'party line': what you have to do to be a 'proper' Christian. Many people in the churches think they are supposed to have beliefs, not questions or doubts. Many outside the churches also assume that. But Christian beliefs are not something we adopt at baptism or confirmation and then file away, like an insurance policy, for the rest of our lives. Believing, according to Christianity, and John's Gospel in particular, is something we *receive and do*. It is a gift and a choice, like the experience of friendship, or falling in love and eventually getting married. John's Gospel strongly emphasizes both aspects. To believe is to trust and obey. Yet we can't make ourselves trust another person – or God, for that matter. We don't trust someone – even God – because they say 'trust me'. Trust must somehow be created.

Here, in the conclusion, John has stated his purpose in writing; 'that you may believe that Jesus is the Christ, the Son of God'. Here are two titles that have always expressed what Christians came to believe about Jesus of Nazareth. He was the 'Christ', the expected Messiah – that is, God's anointed one. Jewish beliefs about the Messiah varied, some emphasizing a military, nationalistic deliverer, others a more spiritual and supernatural figure.

---

9 John's Gospel has three ways of talking about believing: believe *that* – that is, believe that God sent Jesus, and everything that follows from that; believe *in* – that is, believe in Jesus or his name; believe – a shorthand expression for either or both of the other two.

But varied though these expectations were, common to them all was the conviction that the Messiah, or God with the Messiah as God's agent, would usher in God's new age; that would be his task.

'Son of God' was a title with even greater potential for spelling out the significance and identity of Jesus. In the Jewish world into which Jesus was born, 'son' could denote not only origin, but also character, as in 'sons of thunder' (Mark 3.17), or destiny, as in 'son of perdition' (John 17.12). So 'Son of God' expressed where Jesus came from, who he was like, and where he was going.

Who was John writing for? That's not as obvious as *why* he wrote, since he tells us that. Did he write for people who were Christians, to confirm them in the faith they already had? Or was it to bring people who were not Christians to faith? The crucial word in 20.31 is written in two ways in our oldest manuscripts, and could mean either 'go on believing' or 'come to believe'. But the Gospel reads very much like an 'in-house' document, especially in what the writer assumes his readers already know. (What he doesn't assume is their knowledge of Aramaic or Hebrew words such as 'Rabbi' (1.38, compare 1.41–42, 9.7), since he takes the trouble to explain them).

So the Gospel ends where it began – with its message of life. And the source of that life, as the writer seems never to tire of insisting, is the 'name' of Jesus – his authority, character and very being, all of which bear the authority, character and being of God.

Summary

In this chapter, taking our cue from John's prologue and conclusion, we have tried to set the scene. We have looked at the Gospel from three perspectives, each giving complementary views of the Gospel. The story of the mission of a 'Son' highlights his origin and destiny: he comes from God and returns to God. It tells of the gifts he brings: above all, life and light. Some welcome these gifts, others do not. But this very opposition becomes the means for the supreme revelation of the glory of both Father and Son. In this way the mission is accomplished, and the mission goes on.

This mission is at the same time a drama: a poignant drama about the source and nature of truth, no less, and, as such, shot through with irony. Some think they know, and they do not; others, unwittingly, testify to the truth. And so this mission of God to the world, permeated as it is by tragic irony, becomes also the story of 'judgement', a word we need to understand in John's terms. God's light has entered our darkness, showing up the darkness for what it is. God's love has embraced the world, and that love – nothing else – *is* the judgement. But it means that decisions and choices have to be made: where does the truth lie, and will humankind choose 'light' or 'darkness'?

But though judgement – present and future – is the inescapable downside of the coming of the light, we should not forget that the Church quickly came to regard John's writing as a 'Gospel': in keeping with the purpose of the author:

> These things have been written so that you may come to believe that Jesus is the Messiah, the Son of God, and that through be-lieving you may have life through his name. (20.31)

John's story is the story of Love's invitation to Life.

2

The Puzzle of John

An elusive author

If we are to appreciate how extraordinary the Gospel of John is –
and by 'extraordinary' I really mean how rich and profound it is –
we shall need to get beneath its surface. And that means a little
detective work is in order. We naturally assume that a man called
John wrote this Gospel, because that is what our New Testaments
tell us: 'the Gospel according to Saint John' – presumably John, son
of Zebedee and brother of James. Yet this title – 'superscription', to
give it its proper name – was only added later, after the Gospel was
written and published. So, once we have subtracted the title, it is obvious that the Gospel was written anonymously; the author's name
does not occur at all. In this respect, it is like the other Gospels.

So is the title 'the Gospel according to Saint John' mistaken?
Not necessarily. But this is why we must examine the evidence
as carefully as we can. We need to begin at the end, with chapter 21. Most scholars think that this chapter was added shortly
after the Gospel was finished. As we saw in Chapter 1, the last
two verses of chapter 20 (vv. 30–31), read like the original conclusion. It's as if the orchestra has stopped playing, we are about
to applaud, and it starts up again.

'The Beloved Disciple'

Chapter 21 identifies the author of the Gospel as 'the disciple
whom Jesus loved'. A story involving this disciple, together with

Jesus and Simon Peter, has just been recounted (21.15–23); the writer goes on:

> This is the disciple who is testifying to these things and has written them, and we know that his testimony is true. But there are also many other things that Jesus did; if everyone of them were written down, I suppose that the world itself could not contain the books that would be written.' (vv. 24–25)

We tend to assume that the writer here is referring to John. Who else could it be? Wasn't he often with Peter? They are together, for example, in Acts 3 and 4, and the two of them, together with John's brother, James, seem to have constituted an inner circle among Jesus' 12 disciples (for example Mark 5.37). But the evidence as a whole is rather more tantalizing and mysterious.

At the Last Supper

So was this anonymous disciple whom Jesus loved – scholars refer to him as the 'Beloved Disciple' – really John or not? This disciple appears in the Gospels only four – possibly five – times. The first occasion is the Last Supper (13.23–26). We must picture the scene. Everyone would be reclining at an angle to the table, as they did in those days, each resting on their left elbow and using their free right hand to eat with. So 'the disciple whom Jesus loved' would be on Jesus' left; all he would need to do to talk to Jesus would be to lean back. Peter, presumably, was on the Beloved Disciple's left, and all *he* had to do was to lean back as well. That seems straightforward enough. It is the sequel that is puzzling. Jesus responds to the disciples' request by revealing the identity of the traitor (vv. 26–27). So why does the writer say, after Jesus has handed the bread to Judas and told him to do what he had to do, 'Now no one at the table knew why he said this to him' (v. 28)?

Why doesn't the Beloved Disciple take any action? Presumably he – or he and Peter – could have wrestled Judas to the ground? Even if they baulked at doing that in front of Jesus, could they not have followed Judas out of the upper room? It's as if the exchanges between Peter, the Beloved Disciple and Jesus had never taken place. In fact, if someone were to remove verses 23–25 from our New Testaments, it wouldn't be obvious that anything was missing.

The other detail here, which many commentators have noticed, is the way in which the author describes the position of 'the disciple whom Jesus loved': literally, 'on the bosom of Jesus' (vv. 23, 25). This is how the Gospel described the position of 'the Son': 'in the bosom of the Father' (1.18). Is it fanciful to think that the repetition of the same image is deliberate? The author may want us to see that the Beloved Disciple is to Jesus as Jesus is to God. (This might be a good reason for thinking that this disciple is this Gospel's origin and inspiration, but stands at one remove from its actual composition.)

There is one awkward question to consider here. We can't simply dismiss the notion that the relationship between Jesus and this disciple was a gay relationship just because many would be offended, even scandalized, by the idea. We can, however, reject it on the grounds that it would have been extremely improbable. It is difficult to imagine that two Jewish men would have had such a relationship, since it was forbidden by their Scriptures. It is also highly unlikely that it would have been overlooked or forgotten in the young Christian Church, which continued to condemn homosexual practice.[1]

At the foot of the cross

'The disciple whom Jesus loved' next appears in the Gospel at Jesus' crucifixion. There is an earlier reference to an 'other disciple', known to the high priest who, with Peter, followed Jesus after his arrest (18.15–16); he may have been the Beloved Disciple, but the Gospel doesn't say so. But the Beloved Disciple is explicitly mentioned in a scene at the foot of the cross:

---

1 Christian condemnation of contemporary homosexual practices are reflected in Romans 1.26–27; 1 Corinthians 6.9 and 1 Timothy 1.10.

When Jesus saw his mother and the disciple whom he loved standing beside her, he said to his mother, 'Woman, this is your son.' Then he said to the disciple, 'Here is your mother.' And from that hour the disciple took her into his own home. (19.26–27)

This is an attractive picture, and I hesitate to raise questions about it. Readers of John's Gospel can, and do, take this as it stands, but, as we shall go on seeing throughout this book, there is often more to John's narratives than first meets the eye. If this is an accurate picture of what happened, it raises questions about the other Gospels. They all say that the women – the mother of Jesus not being one of them – stood at some distance from the cross. That is far more likely. Even in the unlikely event of Roman soldiers allowing them anywhere near the cross, the fact that Jesus would have been completely naked makes it extremely improbable that any woman – except his mother? – would have approached. Whatever actually happened, John's Gospel is the only one to say that the mother of Jesus was present; the only woman mentioned directly or indirectly – Luke 23.49 refers back to Luke 8.2–3 – in all four Gospels is Mary Magdalene.

If there is a deeper meaning in this simple family scene, what is it? There are two clues. Jesus here is using the language of adoption. There is an example of such language in the Apocrypha (1 Maccabees 2.65) where Mattathias, on the point of death, makes provision for his children by declaring, 'Look, your brother Simon shall be your father.'[2] So Jesus here is designating 'the disciple he loved' as his successor; from now on that disciple is the son of Jesus' mother (who also is anonymous in this Gospel) and, similarly, she will be his mother.

This is the first clue. Adoption language shows that a new relationship is being forged. But the other clue to the meaning of this scene lies in the way in which, in this Gospel, characters

2 Andrew T. Lincoln, *The Gospel According to St John*, London: Continuum, 2005, pp. 476–7.

are often *representative*. So, for example, Nathaniel represents a 'true Israelite' (1.47), Nicodemus 'a teacher of Israel' (3.10), and the blind man who receives his sight a model disciple (9.34, 38). So, as time has passed, the mother of Jesus may have come to represent the Jewish nation and tradition into which Jesus was born, and 'the disciple whom Jesus loved' the representative – almost, the ideal disciple – of the new faith.

This does not mean they are fictitious. Clearly, the mother of Jesus was a real person. And there is no reason to doubt that the disciple whom Jesus loved was a real person, too. But both, in this Gospel, have come to stand for something more – perhaps the old faith and the new – meeting at the foot of the cross.

At the empty tomb

The Beloved Disciple appears a third time in John's Gospel on Easter morning, after Mary Magdalene has found the stone at the entrance to the tomb rolled away and run to find him and Simon Peter. Again, it is natural to think that this unnamed disciple is John, but in the oldest Easter tradition of all the apostle Paul writes that Jesus appeared 'first to Cephas [that is Peter], then to the twelve' (1 Corinthians 15.5, compare Luke 24.34). Whoever the unnamed disciple was, he outruns Peter, peeps into the tomb, but doesn't go in (vv. 4–5). Peter, following behind, does go in (vv. 6–7), and then, says the writer, 'the other disciple, who reached the tomb first, also went in, and he saw and believed' (v. 8). But then, curiously, the writer continues as if he hadn't written those words at all: '*for* as yet *they* [Mary and Peter?] did not understand the scripture that he must rise from the dead. Then the disciples returned to their homes' (vv. 9–10). I have italicized the two words which seem to me to follow on rather oddly from verse 8; the story is like the episode at the Last Supper involving the Beloved Disciple: he is there and not there. Certainly, the story at the empty tomb carries on as if nothing has happened: 'Mary stood weeping outside the tomb . . .' (v. 11). So the Beloved Disciple 'believed', but didn't tell her!

I hope readers will see that I am not exaggerating the difficulties here. The Beloved Disciple is a mysterious, elusive figure. We can't simply dismiss him as fictitious; but, whatever the historical truth, this seems to be further evidence for saying he functions in this Gospel as a model disciple.

By the Sea of Galilee

His final appearance in this Gospel occurs in chapter 21, which was added shortly after the Gospel was completed. A group of disciples in Galilee are fishing; they include disciples prominent in the other Gospels (Simon Peter and the sons of Zebedee, who are not otherwise mentioned by name in this Gospel), two who receive special mentions in John (Thomas and Nathaniel), and two others who are not named (v. 2). A miraculous catch of fish follows the appearance of the risen Christ on the shore and then, when they go ashore, Jesus invites them to a breakfast he has prepared, though he invites them to contribute to the meal as well (vv. 3–6, 9–13). But, in the middle of this story, the disciple whom Jesus loved shows himself a step ahead of Simon Peter; he alone recognizes the stranger on the shore (v. 7), although it's only Peter who then plunges into the lake.

That is all we hear of the Beloved Disciple for the moment. He reappears after the conversation between Jesus and Peter when breakfast is finished. And here, I believe, is a subtle but unmistakable clue to his role as the ideal disciple in this Gospel. Jesus has just said to Peter, 'Follow me' (v. 19); Peter turns and sees the disciple whom Jesus loved doing just that: 'following' (v. 20). The NRSV translates this verse by adding an extra word: 'Then Peter turned and saw the disciple whom Jesus loved following *them*.' The word 'them' is not there in the Greek – which is why I think the writer intends us to see a deeper meaning: this disciple is already doing just what Jesus has commanded Peter to do: *following*. Of course, we are perfectly entitled to understand the word quite literally: he was following just a few metres behind. But the absence of the word 'them', taken with all the other details we have reviewed here, suggests that this disciple is indeed intended to be, in some way, the ideal disciple. One final detail may point the same way. Jesus, speaking of the Beloved Disciple, says to Peter; 'If it is my will that he remain until I come, what is that to you?' (v. 23c). The word 'remain' here is an important word in this Gospel, being the word used in the last discourses of 'abiding' in the Son and the Father (for example 15.4). So, like the hint about the Beloved Disciple 'following', this reference to him 'abiding' until Jesus comes may be yet another clue that this mysterious figure does indeed function in this Gospel as a model disciple.

Conclusion

It's time to bring the detective work to a close. Some readers may feel I have exaggerated the mystery surrounding 'the disciple whom Jesus loved'. I am not urging any particular point of view, but highlighting the evidence and, above all, the fact that this disciple is never named. It is possible that the disciple was John the son of Zebedee. But the big differences between this Gospel and the others are difficult to explain if John was indeed the writer of this Gospel. Why leave out all the events at which he was a privileged spectator – for example, the transfiguration? Perhaps John was the main inspiration behind the Gospel, which was the product of a long life of reflection on the identity and significance of Jesus.

But the most important point of all about 'the disciple whom Jesus loved' has yet to be mentioned, and with that we shall, for the time being, leave this mystery. People have spoken of this disciple as if he were a special favourite of Jesus, and it may seem natural to understand the words in that way: 'the disciple whom Jesus loved'. But this Gospel, more than once, says that Jesus loved all the disciples (13.1, 34). Is it not possible that the writer is inviting us, the reader, to identify with this anonymous disciple, and to write ourselves into the story? The Beloved Disciple thus becomes a role model for every reader and, at the same time, a promise that we, too, are loved.

John and the other Gospels

Imagine three jigsaw puzzles, each in its own box, one smaller than the other two. The boxes tell you that each jigsaw carries the same picture. Eventually, you complete all three, and you can see for yourself: each jigsaw has enough pieces similar to those in the other two to confirm the accuracy of the label on the box. You can now see that the three jigsaw puzzles, despite the differences of detail, carry basically the same picture. You open the box of a fourth jigsaw. You see only a few pieces which you recognize from the other three. By the time you have completed this fourth jigsaw, you can identify a few sections whose similarity to the other three is clear – but only a few sections.

The analogy with the Gospels is not perfect but, I hope, not unhelpful. At the risk of oversimplifying, I shall set out the 'jigsaw pieces' of John's Gospel in three groups. The details will fill out and complement the three perspectives of the Gospel as the story of a mission, a drama and a trial offered in the previous chapter. Our approach will be a broad-brush approach, with some extra details provided in the footnotes – for those readers with a particular penchant for jigsaws.

The pieces of John found in the other Gospels

The big 'pieces' comprise the following:

- the cleansing of the Temple (2.13–19)
- the feeding of the five thousand and Jesus walking on the water (6.1–21, though the second of these miracles doesn't feature in Luke)
- the anointing of Jesus (12.1–8)
- his entry into Jerusalem (12.12–15)
- the prediction of Judas' betrayal and of Peter's denial (13.21–30, 36–38)
- the arrest, trial and crucifixion of Jesus (chapters 18—19)
- the miraculous catch of fish (21.1–14 – oddly like the story in Luke 5.1–11)

- though Mary Magdalene is mentioned as being at the empty tomb, she is accompanied by other women, and the story of John 20.1–18 is entirely missing.

In all of these stories, shared by John with Matthew, Mark and Luke, there are differences of detail, as well as indications of what John himself understood them to mean. For example, only John says that Jesus used a 'whip of cords' (2.15) in the cleansing of the Temple, and only John has the reference to the little boy with the five loaves and two fish (6.8–9) in the feeding of the five thousand. As for John's account of Jesus' arrest, trial and crucifixion, the differences between John and the other Gospels are very considerable. Sometimes, too, John puts a story in a quite different place: the cleansing of the Temple at the beginning of Jesus' ministry, not the end, and the miraculous catch of fish after the resurrection, whereas in Luke (5.1–11) this story seems to replace the call of the disciples as narrated by Mark (Mark 1.14–18).

This list could be a little longer: there are borderline cases where the differences between John and the other Gospels are greater. The healing of the ruler's son (4.46–54) is rather like the healing of the centurion's son (Matthew 8.5–13; Luke 7.1–10), and Mary Magdalene goes to the empty tomb in the other Gospels, though only in John does the risen Jesus appear to her on her own (20.1–18. Jesus appeared to her and to 'the other Mary' in Matthew 28.9). But now we look at the 'pieces' in our second category.

The pieces of John not in the other Gospels

They make a long list:

- the prologue to the Gospel (1.1–18)
- the wedding at Cana (2.1–11)
- the story of Nicodemus and the teaching which follows (3.1–21)
- Jesus and John the Baptist (3.22–36)
- Jesus and the Samaritan woman (4.1–42)

- the healing of the lame man, and the teaching which follows (5.1–47)
- Jesus' teaching about the bread of life and its sequel (6.22–71)
- the unbelief of Jesus' brothers, and controversies in Jerusalem (7.1–52)
- more controversies with the Pharisees and 'the Jews' (8.12–59)
- the healing of a blind man and, through controversy, his subsequent conversion (9.1–41)
- teaching about the Good Shepherd and more controversies in Jerusalem (10.1–42)
- the raising of Lazarus and the subsequent plot to kill Jesus (11.1–53)
- Jesus' withdrawal from Judaea (11.54–57)
- the plot against Lazarus (12.9–11)
- Greeks look for Jesus (12.20–36)
- the unbelief of 'the Jews' (12.44–50)
- Jesus washes his disciples' feet (13.1–20)
- the farewell discourses and prayer of Jesus (13—17)
- Jesus' appearance to Mary Magdalene at the empty tomb, and his appearance to Thomas (20.1–18, 24–29)
- Jesus, Simon Peter, and the Beloved Disciple (21.15–25).

However, just as, in the last category, we had to note important differences from the other Gospels, so here we note the occasional similarities with the other Gospels, and echoes of them. So Jesus' words to Nicodemus about being 'born again' (John 3.3) are a bit like his saying about the need to become 'like little children' (Matthew 18.3), and his remark to the disciples in Samaria about fields 'ripe for harvesting' (John 4.35) recalls his words about a plentiful harvest in other Gospels (Matthew 9.37; Luke 10.2). These are just two among many examples of words and phrases which occur in the other Gospels, or which are similar to details in the others. And, as we shall note below, one or two of the stories listed in this group of 'pieces' have both similarities with, and dissimilarities from, stories in Matthew, Mark and Luke.

Pieces in John's Gospel like and unlike those in the other Gospels

In many ways this third category raises the most questions, and it's not always easy to decide whether a piece should be listed here, or in one of the other two categories:

- the testimony of John the Baptist to Jesus, and Jesus' coming to John (1.19–34)
- the call of the disciples (1.35–51)
- the woman taken in adultery (7.53—8.11, a late addition to the Gospel)
- the anointing of Jesus (12.1–8)
- the quotation from Isaiah, used by Matthew, Mark and Luke (Matthew 13.15; Mark 4.12; Acts 28.26–27)
- the appearance of the risen Jesus to his disciples (20.19–23, compare Luke 24.36–49).

This third category raises a number of questions. If the writer was an eyewitness, why is his version so different from the others? Even if he wasn't, how do we reconcile his account with those of the others? Or is it a mistake to try? We shall look at an example, which will help us to engage with these questions.

Making sense of the differences

It's tempting to call John 1.35–51 'the call of the disciples' because, at first sight, that is what it appears to be. But this evangelist has a different agenda. He is more interested in the gradual revelation of who Jesus is, and the call of the disciples becomes a 'peg' to hang that on. So, though there are echoes of the call of the disciples in Mark 1.16–20, in fact only Simon Peter and Andrew appear here (not James and John). And only to Philip does Jesus say 'Follow me' (1.43).

We might wonder whether John's version of the disciples' call recounts what happened before Mark's version of events, or whether it was later. Did this early encounter pave the way for the later call by the Sea of Galilee? Or did this confirm the earlier call? These are simply the wrong questions to ask – and quite unnecessary. John is not easily matched up with the other Gospels. For example, Jesus gives Simon his new name of 'Peter' ('Cephas' in Aramaic) here at the start of his ministry (John 1.42), whereas in Matthew it occurs much later (Matthew 16.13–20). So a likely explanation of the differences is that original historical events have been blended with later reflection and interpretation.

This is the best way to make sense of these, and other, differences between John and the other Gospels. The often-cited analogy of four people reporting the same football match differently might account for a few of the differences, but not the majority of them. It is much more probable that each evangelist had his own 'agenda'. If there is an analogy in the world of journalism, it lies in the way in which the Gospel writers seem to have edited the various traditions about Jesus available to them. So here, John may well have adapted earlier traditions about the call of the disciples into a 'weave' of his own.

There are a few more examples in John of stories like and unlike stories in the other Gospels: the healing of the ruler's son, which we noted earlier (John 4.43–54, compare Matthew 8.5–13 and Luke 7.1–10); the healing of the man lying beside the pool of Bethzatha (John 5.1–9, where Jesus' command to the man in verse 8 is almost exactly the same as his command to the paralysed man in Mark 2.11); similarly, the healing of the blind man in John 9.1–7 is a bit like the healing of the blind man in Mark 8.22–26.

It is possible – even probable – that Jesus performed similar miracles, and repeated himself at times. Why not give the same command to two men unable to walk? I am not concerned here with 'explaining' everything – as if that could easily be done anyway. I simply want to urge that we set aside two particular ways of looking at all these differences between John and the other Gospels, because, in my view, they are mistaken. The first is to regard John's Gospel as, more or less, an eyewitness account of Jesus' ministry; as I have suggested, it is not as straightforward as that. The other is to try to harmonize the Gospels so that they make, as it were, one complete jigsaw. This doesn't work, and the Church, interestingly, set its face against this approach as long ago as the second century.[3]

I imagine that by now some readers may have had enough of this discussion.[4] After all, does it really matter? But perhaps it is better to ask: do we want to understand John's Gospel more fully, and appreciate more deeply his message? And to do that it can be helpful at least to consider what John was trying to do. Was he correcting the other Gospels (if we assume John was writing later)? This seems a startling idea. But John does say that John the Baptist wasn't Elijah (John 1.21, contrast for example Mark 9.13), and that he had not yet been imprisoned when Jesus began his own ministry (John 3.24, contrast Mark 1.14). Such possible 'corrections', however, are very few and far between. So this seems unlikely.

If John wasn't correcting the other Gospels, was he trying to complement them in some way, making good what he thought was missing? This is more plausible – though we can't be sure whether or not he knew the other Gospels – or some version of them. But we're still left wondering why there are *some* overlaps and, perhaps, why there are no parables, no exorcisms, and hardly any teaching at all referring to 'the Kingdom of God' (John 3.3 and 5 are the only examples).

Two suggestions

So what was John up to? I conclude this section with two suggestions. First, John carried on where the other Gospel writers left off. This suggestion was made by the great Roman Catholic scholar Raymond Brown, and I think it has a lot to commend it.

---

3 Tatian's *Diatessaron* in the second century was an early attempt to harmonize the Gospels but, despite the awkward questions which the differences between the Gospels posed, the Christian Church has accepted a four-Gospel canon.

4 Many of John's 'seams', where he links one major section of his Gospel with another, sometimes seem to echo the other Gospels, for example 4.43–45 and 10.19–21.

In arguing that John carried on where the other Gospels leave off, I do not mean that John's Gospel contains no early traditions about Jesus. It almost certainly does; many scholars have concluded that it has information about Jesus not found in the other Gospels. But John was almost certainly writing later than the other three.[5] He and his community had even more Christian experience and mature reflection to bring to their task. So for example, he begins three sections of his Gospel with miracle stories like those in the other Gospels (5.1–9; 6.1–21; 9.1–7), but moves on to long discourses or prolonged conversations explaining what these 'signs' point to, or, in chapter 9, showing how the healed man came to believe in Jesus. This story, especially, is thought to reflect a later stage of the conflicts and controversies which developed between the early Christian communities and the Jewish communities of which they were originally part (on this, see below).

My second suggestion is closely linked to the first. In carrying on where the other Gospels leave off, John has made more explicit what is often only implicit, or lightly touched upon, in his predecessors. For example, the Son of Man sayings in the other Gospels are different and more cryptic, from those in John. In Matthew, Mark and Luke Jesus three times declares that the Son of Man must 'undergo great suffering' and be 'handed over' (for example Mark 8.31; 9.31; 10.33–34). John's Gospel keeps the word 'must' (which means here 'part of God's purpose'), but instead of language about suffering and betrayal, he has the word 'lift up': 'just as Moses lifted up the serpent in the wilderness, so must the Son of Man be lifted up' (3.14, compare the crowd's question at 12.34).

Above all, John majors on the identity of Jesus, and particularly his relationship to God. The other Gospels have surprisingly few references to Jesus as the Son of God, whereas in John Jesus frequently refers to himself as 'the Son'. In John, too, Jesus is far more explicit about who he is, notably in the so-called 'I am' sayings (discussed in Chapter 5: for example, 'I am the bread of

---

5 Few scholars have followed John Robinson in his argument in *The Priority of John*, London: SCM, 1985.

life' (John 6.35, 48). Most important of all, John seems to make more explicit the belief that Jesus was divine. This prompts the question which must be the subject of our next section.

Is John's Jesus the real Jesus?

We should face this question head-on. Jesus in John speaks in a different way, and says different things from the Jesus of the parables and the Sermon on the Mount. Most striking of all, in Matthew, Mark and Luke Jesus rarely speaks directly about himself; in John, to put it rather provocatively, Jesus is always talking about himself! But before we address this question directly, it might be useful to summarize the argument so far.

In section 1 of this Chapter we saw that 'the disciple whom Jesus loved' is anonymous – and, presumably, deliberately so. Not only that, the final version of the Gospel seems to be the product of a community: *we* saw' (1.14), *we* know' (21.24). At the same time, there is plenty of evidence to suggest that John's Gospel grew out of genuine memories about a real person, 'the Word made flesh': a man who really lived and who really died. So we can be relaxed about whether there is a historical bedrock to this Gospel, and ask instead the question which the evangelist and his community want us to ask: *is their testimony true?*

In the last section we surveyed the similarities and differences between John and the other Gospels, concluding that John, like Matthew, Mark and Luke, had his own particular agenda in writing. His agenda is even more Christ-centred than theirs, carrying on, in a sense, where they leave off, and making more explicit what they sometimes only foreshadow or imply.

History, or testimony rooted in history?

So there are two different ways of approaching the question 'is John's Jesus the real Jesus?' We could treat it as a historical question: has John given us a historically accurate portrait of Jesus. But, then, was that what the author set out to do? And, anyway, we could ask the same question of the other Gospels, or of the biography of any historical figure: 'Is this the real—?'

There is a different way of tackling our question – and I am urging that this is what John and his community would want us to do. The more important question to ask is this: can the testimony of this Gospel be believed? Its testimony is far more than historical facts, though it clearly contains them. But it testifies, above all, to the truth behind the facts.

We might still feel that John's Jesus is so different from, say, the Jesus of Luke that we can't help wondering how reliable a picture it is. It helps, I believe, to realize that the writers of our four Gospels used their imaginations (as did most, if not all, the people who wrote the books of the Bible). Most Christian preachers and teachers do the same – and rightly so – in retelling Bible stories. We might say, 'That's all right for us, but weren't the evangelists telling it how it really was?'

But what matters, then and now, is the *faithful* use of our imagination: being faithful to the gospel in a way that nurtures or creates faith in those who hear our preaching, or read the Gospels. So we are not talking here about a writer letting his imagination run riot. (Some of the Gospels that didn't get into the New Testament are examples of this.) Rather, this is a writer who has placed his sanctified imagination at the service of the gospel.

So, in exploring the question 'Is John's Jesus the real Jesus?', we are looking at how John has chosen to tell the story of Jesus, including his version of the teaching of Jesus and what Jesus says about himself in John. We shall look at each of these in turn.

The words of Jesus in John

Years ago, I led a Bible study on John's Gospel, and took the bull by the horns at the outset: I suggested that not all the words attributed to Jesus in John were spoken by him. Members of the group, understandably, found that difficult. I should not have started there at all. I discussed this question with another minister, arguing that what really mattered was not whether it was Jesus who said (for example), 'I am the light of the world', but that these words are in the Bible. My colleague thought that the words would have more authority for the Christian if they had been spoken by Jesus.

On further reflection, I came to believe that my colleague's argument was a circular one. A Christian comes to the New Testament already accepting its authority (even though there are very different understandings of its authority). So she is unlikely to say that 'I am the light of the world' is *more likely* to be true if Jesus said it; she will believe that already. Conversely, someone who does not yet share the Christian faith will not be persuaded that Jesus is the light of the world by being told that Jesus made that claim for himself.

We need to begin where the Gospel begins: 'the Word made flesh'. Jesus really lived, taught and healed. So we can be relaxed at the thought that, in John's Gospel in particular, the words of Jesus are extended by later Christian reflection. His original teaching shades into the subsequent reflection. Sometimes it is reworded and reshaped, so that we can't see 'the join', and we don't need to; it's all inspired Scripture. We are in good hands – those of the inspired, gifted writer of this Gospel; under his deeply spiritual guidance, we shall not stray far.

One example may help. We can well imagine that the writer thought often about the prayers of Jesus: traditions about how Jesus himself had prayed, and of what Jesus had taught about prayer during his earthly life. But, given their belief in Jesus' ascension to heaven, is it not likely that they would reflect also about his continuing prayer in heaven? It is clear from other New Testament writers that Jesus' 'intercession' in heaven was part of the faith from the very beginning (Romans 8.34; Hebrews 7.25; 1 John 2.1). So John 17, the 'high priestly' prayer of Jesus, is likely to be the product of not only memories of what Jesus said and did about prayer, but also the writer's later reflection about Jesus' ministry of prayer in heaven. The prayer of Jesus in John 17 sounds, sometimes, as though Jesus is already in heaven ('And now I am no longer in the world' (v. 11)) and, sometimes, as though he is on the very threshold of heaven ('But now I am coming to you' (v. 13)). In any case, it is hard to think that anyone would have overheard this prayer. The other Gospels say Jesus took three disciples with him into Gethsemane, that he went forward a little way, and they fell asleep.

This prayer, in fact, is a good example of John carrying on where the other Gospels leave off. The other Gospels report that Jesus, just before his arrest, prayed that 'the cup' might pass from him (thus, Mark 14.35–36; Matthew 26.39; Luke 22.42; John 12.27 seems to be an echo). They imply, without expressly saying so, that, as he wrestled in prayer for hours, he moved to a profound acceptance of God's will. It's as if John gives us the outcome of Jesus' long hours of prayer (silent, perhaps, more than spoken): 'Father, the hour has come; glorify your Son so that the Son may glorify you' (John 17.1).

We can only speculate about the author's sources but, just as it is unlikely that there was anyone there to hear the prayer of Jesus in the garden before his arrest, so the evangelist would not have known what conversation took place between Jesus and Pilate. (The four Gospels differ about the details of this anyway.)

There is another reason for seeing the work of the Gospel writer here. Jesus, both here and almost everywhere else in this Gospel, uses many of the same words and phrases which occur in another New Testament book bearing the same name – the First Letter of John. So, for example, the writer of 1 John says: 'All who obey his commandments abide in him, and he abides in them' (1 John 3.24a, compare John 15.10). Passages such as 1 John 2.8b; 3.24; 4.9 provide more examples of John-like language, while 1 John 5.4 and 9 are also like words attributed to Jesus in John's Gospel. This could mean that the writer of 1 John copied the language and style of Jesus as reported in John's Gospel. But that is unlikely, because Jesus in the other three Gospels speaks so differently; most obviously, he speaks about the Kingdom of God or (more often in Matthew), about the Kingdom of heaven, whereas in John, 'eternal life' seems to replace Kingdom language. It is more probable that John's Gospel and 1 John come from the same early Christian 'school', each putting their own distinctive stamp on the teaching of Jesus and the traditions about him.

The teaching of Jesus in John

So we come to what Jesus says about himself in John's Gospel. Here the picture is so different from the other Gospels, that I do not see how we can have it both ways. Admittedly, Mark may have heightened the mystery and secrecy surrounding Jesus' Messiahship, but in the other Gospels Jesus says little about himself; for example, he hardly ever refers to himself as 'the Son' – only Mark 13.32 and Matthew 11.27 (Luke 10.22), and there are none of the 'I am' sayings. There is, however – and this is important – the reassurance he gives to the disciples in the story of his walking on the water: 'Take heart, it is I; do not be afraid' (Mark 6.50; Matthew 14.27). As we shall see (Chapter 5), the Greek words for 'it is I', *ego eimi*, could have deeper resonances.

So in the other Gospels Jesus is portrayed as being reticent about himself – until his trial, and even there, according to Matthew and Luke (Matthew 26.64; Luke 22. 67–68), Jesus declines to say whether he is the Messiah or not, though he does speak of a coming 'Son of Man'. In Mark, Jesus responds to the question of whether he is the Messiah by saying 'I am' (*ego eimi* again, Mark 14.61–62), though here, too, a few manuscripts portray him as being more ambivalent.

Whatever Jesus did or did not say at his trial, the difference between John and the other Gospels is very clear in their varying accounts of his earlier teaching. Apart from Matthew 14.33, it is not until Simon Peter's confession midway through the other Gospels (Mark 8.29; Matthew 16.16; Luke 9.20) that the disciples had any inkling of who Jesus was. By contrast, in John's Gospel, Andrew informs Peter, 'We have found the Messiah,' at the very outset of their discipleship (1.41).

So, by reflecting on and developing Jesus' original teaching, and in reflecting on and making more explicit what Jesus had implied about himself, the writer of John's Gospel has carried on where Matthew, Mark and Luke left off. Of course, this way of putting things must not be taken too literally, or pressed too hard; the ways and the work of the four Gospel writers may have criss-crossed and overlapped in many ways we simply don't know about. But it certainly seems that John carried on early reflection about who Jesus was, and particularly his relationship to 'the Father'.

So if the historical Jesus spoke of himself as an unassuming 'Son of Man', whereas John's Jesus says 'I am the One', does this mean that the later doctrine of the divinity of Jesus was a Christian invention? 'Invention' is a loaded word. It would be more true to say that belief in the divinity of Jesus developed gradually as the early Christians reflected on how God was changing the world – and people's lives – through the life, death and resurrection of Jesus. So John's testimony is not an example of a Christian imagination run riot or of an arbitrary addition to earlier beliefs about a human Jesus. It is John dotting 'Is' and crossing 'Ts' – making more explicit what before had been largely implicit about Jesus: he had come from God, and he returned to God.

A personal testimony

If I may be permitted a personal testimony towards the end of a discussion that some readers may have found difficult: I have learned so much more from this Gospel by allowing it to be broken open, in the way I have tried to do here, than I could ever have done if I had continued to read it in a more one-dimensional way as a straightforward record of what Jesus said and did. But far better than my testimony are the thoughts of a great biblical teacher of the third century, Origen.

Origen encouraged people to distinguish between what he called 'the flesh' and 'the soul' of Scripture. By the flesh of Scripture Origen meant its superficial sense or the external events narrated by each writer. So he asks, with reference to Genesis 1, whether 'anyone of sense' will really think that there was a first, second or third day without sun, moon or stars. Even the Gospels, he suggests, are full of similar details. For example, how could the devil have shown Jesus all the kingdoms of the world from one high mountain? He concludes that Scripture has a 'body' which can be seen, and a soul and spirit which can't be seen. But it is the soul, or spirit, of Scripture which nourishes the reader.[6]

Origen's words seem eminently applicable to John's Gospel. This Gospel's preferred word for what we call a 'miracle' is 'sign': the outward event points to an inward truth. The feeding of the five thousand points to Jesus the bread of life (John 6.1–15, 35); the raising of Lazarus points forward to the resurrection of Jesus, and is a sign that Jesus is the resurrection and the life (11.25). What really nourishes the soul is following where the sign points: believing that Jesus turned water into wine doesn't get us very far – though I am not arguing here that he did not. What really matters is seeing that the first sign 'at Cana in Galilee' has become, in the expert hands of the evangelist, a parable of Jesus' entire ministry: turning the water of human life into the wine of God's eternal life.[7]

The journey which this Gospel invites us to travel will, I believe, be illuminated by considering the journey which the author himself might have travelled. We shall need to use our imaginations a little in reconstructing that journey – but we can do that, I hope, in a way that is faithful to the mysterious document which was the product of that journey.

The journey of the Beloved Disciple

'The disciple whom Jesus loved', as we saw earlier in this chapter, is a mysterious, elusive figure: anonymous and, perhaps, inclusive, drawing us as the readers into the story of Jesus. But there is no reason to doubt that he was a real person: the testimony of the community behind chapter 21 ('this is the disciple who is testifying to these things and has written them, and we know that his witness is true', v. 24) makes that clear.

---

6 From the *Philokalia* of Origen, quoted in A. C. Bouquet's *A Lectionary of Christian Prose*, London: Longman's Green and Co. Ltd, 1939, pp. 9–10.

7 The word usually translated 'first' in 2.11 is not the usual Greek word for 'first' (*protos*), but the word *arche* (literally, 'beginning'). This might suggest that John saw the turning of water into wine as the archetype of all Jesus' 'signs'.

Let us suppose that it was John, the son of Zebedee. We can't prove this, and it is difficult to think that John, however inspired, singlehandedly wrote the Gospel in the form it has come down to us. But if we act on the principle of 'no smoke without fire', recalling the early Christian tradition that John was indeed the author of this Gospel then we might begin to imagine something of his life's journey.

A leader in Jerusalem

The journey begins in or around Jerusalem. For whatever reason, the ministry of Jesus in Galilee is far less prominent in John, and therefore so is the journey, as narrated by the other Gospels, of the twelve disciples, including John, from Galilee to Jerusalem. But we know from the Acts of the Apostles that Jerusalem is where the Church began, even if the first disciples also saw the risen Jesus in Galilee. It also seems that the first followers of Jesus – not yet called 'Christians' – made a corner of the Temple precinct, Solomon's portico, their own (Acts 5.12). Other Jewish sects, including a 'cell' of Essenes, did the same. So it is possible that, while Peter and Paul went on their travels, and James, the brother of Jesus, assumed overall leadership of the church in Jerusalem (Galatians 2.7, 11; Acts 15.13, 19), John continued to lead a Christian group of his own.

Over the next half-century, John and his community, we may suppose, treasured their memories of Jesus, but did not simply pass on these traditions word-for-word. They reflected on them in the light of their own experiences. If they lived in or near Jerusalem and if, as is likely, they were engaged in controversy and sometimes sharp conflict with their Jewish contemporaries, that would help to explain the 'Jewish flavour' of this Gospel, and its mostly Jerusalem-centred storyline. To repeat: this does not mean John has 'made it all up': it *does* mean (I am suggesting) that everything has been refracted through the lens of his and his community's experiences.

Many scholars cite as an example of this the expulsion of the once-blind man from the synagogue (John 9.22, 34). The wording of verse 22 in this story – and 12.42 is similar – seems to reflect a later period, not the lifetime of Jesus himself: 'for the Jews had already agreed that anyone who confessed Jesus to be the Messiah would be put out of the synagogue'. According to the other Gospels – Mark in particular – the Messiahship of Jesus was a secret, which even the twelve disciples were slow to grasp. And there is nothing in Acts about Christians being expelled from synagogues. According to John 16.2, Jesus predicted that this is what would happen. But that would be natural in a farewell discourse of this kind. Again and again in the Bible a great leader or teacher is portrayed as warning his descendants or followers what would happen to them after he was no longer with them.

So we should not be surprised if the many discussions – and arguments – which John and his community had with their fellow Jews have coloured and shaped this Gospel. This happened in the writing of the other Gospels, especially Matthew, but not as clearly or as much as in the writing of John. Jesus himself, of course, was engaged in controversy with Jewish leaders in Jerusalem. They asked him by what authority he did what he was doing (Mark 11.28; Matthew 21.23; Luke 20.2); interestingly, a question very like that one comes near the beginning of John (2.18). It is possible that people were already asking, in Jesus' own lifetime, whether he was the Messiah, and whether anything good could come out of Nazareth or Bethlehem (for example John 7.41), but the inhabitants of Jerusalem would certainly have gone on asking those questions after Jesus' death and resurrection, as more of their number became followers of Jesus.

So this might be called Stage 1 of the journey of the disciple whom Jesus loved: geographically he travelled little, but spiritually he travelled far, as he wrestled with all the questions which these controversies generated: was Jesus really the Messiah, and what did it mean to call him the Son of God?

From Jerusalem to Ephesus

And so to Stage 2 of this disciple's journey. We fast forward from the year 55 to the year 85. A cataclysm has occurred: the

Jewish Roman war of 66–70, culminating in the destruction of Jerusalem and its Temple. Where did John and his community go? We have no hard evidence, but there was a memory that Jesus had warned his disciples to flee when trouble came (for example Mark 13.14). Did they leave Palestine altogether and settle in Ephesus in Asia Minor? This may be the journey behind the tradition remembered by Irenaeus, the second-century bishop of Lyons.[8]

We can only speculate. What is so interesting – and important – is how much more frequent in John's Gospel are references to what we might call the big wide world (the *kosmos*), beyond Palestine. Can it be that this Gospel reflects the broadening, cosmopolitan experiences of John and his community in the years that followed their emigration from their homeland to the much more multicultural environment of Ephesus?

New challenges

If we are on the right lines in imagining a group of Jewish Christian emigrés in Ephesus, we can be quite sure that their new home would have presented them with new challenges and questions. Greek influences would have been greater, and more Greek spoken than in the circles in which they moved in Jerusalem. This move to a more Greek environment might explain why some Christians, thoroughly steeped in such an environment, began to ask whether Jesus had been really, physically human; or, whether, though human, perhaps he had not experienced bloody, humiliating death by crucifixion. We know from the letter in the New Testament which we call 1 John that there were such people: 'Many false prophets have gone out into the world. By this you know the Spirit of God: every spirit that confesses that Jesus Christ has come in the flesh is from God, and every spirit that does not confess Jesus is not from God' (1 John 4.1–2). The

---

8 The relevant passages from Irenaeus are quoted in C. K. Barrett's commentary, *The Gospel According to St John*, 1st edition, London: SPCK, 1955, pp. 83–4.

same concern may lie behind the cryptic references to water and blood in the same letter: 'This is the one who came by water and blood, Jesus Christ, not with water only but with the water and the blood' (1 John 5.6, compare John 19.34–35). So as John – or the self-effacing evangelist who wrote up John's memories and reflections – put the finishing touches to the Gospel, they may have 'topped and tailed' it by emphasizing Jesus really lived and really died. So the prologue stresses that 'the Word was made flesh' (1.14), and 'doubting Thomas' is convinced that the One who has risen is none other than the one who was crucified (20.24–29).

But Greek thought and ideas were not the only challenges to confront John's community. Back home in Jerusalem, Christian communities were not, at first, easily distinguishable from their fellow Jews. Many followers of Jesus would have continued to attend synagogue and keep the laws of Moses; where they continued to be practising Jews, the bone of contention would have been, not whether they kept the Sabbath and refrained from eating pork, but their scandalous belief in a crucified Messiah. Although in Jerusalem Roman military power, as well as the Jewish religious establishment, was never far away, in Ephesus Christians may have felt much more vulnerable. Whenever and wherever Christians began to be expelled from synagogues,[9] they became more exposed not only to Jewish opprobrium, but also to the suspicions of their Greek and Roman contemporaries: who were these strange people, rumoured to engage in a strange ritual which involved drinking blood, and who worshipped Christ as God?

John's Gospel may well have been completed during Domitian's reign (AD 81–96). The Roman writer Suetonius no doubt included a lot of tittle-tattle in his lives of *The Twelve Caesars*. He tells us, for example, that Domitian used to spend hours early on in his reign catching flies. But there can be little doubt that

---

9 When, and even whether, this happened is still hotly disputed by scholars. But there is, as far as I am aware, no evidence for any expulsion of Christians from synagogues in the period before AD 70. The distinction between 'Jew' and 'Christian', so familiar to us, was a long time in coming, belonging to the second century, rather than the first.

he was hated and feared for his cruelty. (The fact that he had himself proclaimed emperor twenty-one times suggests a certain measure of insecurity.)

Scholars still debate how much Domitian persecuted the Christians. Even if he did not, they would have lived in a society which did not readily tolerate 'nonconformists' like them. And nonconformists in the Roman Empire, apart from a few eccentric philosophers, were always in danger of being dubbed subversives. This is the likely background to the words of Jesus' discourse in John 15: 'If the world hates you, be aware that it hated me before it hated you.' All the more remarkable is one of the most famous verses in the entire Gospel: 'For God so loved the world that he gave his only Son . . . ' (3.16).

A Gospel for the world

So I am suggesting that a Gospel whose early life began in the very Jewish environment of Jerusalem, and which in so many ways is a very Jewish document, was completed in the much more cosmopolitan environment of Ephesus. And that can be seen especially in the Gospel's many references to 'the world'.

But, to complete our imaginative reconstruction of the journey of the Beloved Disciple, we need to place two positives alongside the challenges of Greek thought and the intimidating presence of Roman imperial power. The first positive is the evangelistic opportunities. However few or many had been the contacts of John's community with Gentiles back home in Palestine, Ephesus, as the saying goes, was 'something else'. Here was a challenge to rethink the story of Jesus and commend it to a wider audience. Jewish origins and early traditions were not forgotten and John's Gospel remained more Jewish than Greek. But its testimony is clear: 'The true light, which enlightens everyone, was coming into the world' (1.9); 'Here is the Lamb of God who takes away the sin of the world!' (1.29). And a claim for Jesus to rival what Emperor Domitian was asserting about himself: 'We know that this is truly the Saviour of the world' (4.42).

That brings us to the second positive thing to be said about the journey of the disciple which we have been tracing in this section. New challenges and new encounters, faithfully met and overcome, stretch a person's faith. Can this be what happened to John and his community? In the years that followed their flight from Jerusalem, they faced the challenges of Ephesus, the splendours of Greek culture, the attractions and distractions of Greek thought and philosophy. The prologue to the Gospel is the most striking monument to this stretching of their faith. But the Gospel as a whole bears the marks of a writer and of a community which has seen the 'big picture': the inscription above Jesus' cross may well have been written in three languages, 'in Hebrew, in Latin and in Greek', but it is only John who bothers to tell us this (19.20). It is also only John who has reference to 'some Greeks' who want to see Jesus (12.20), a story which ends with another of this Gospel's universal vistas: 'And I, when I am lifted up from the earth, will draw all people to myself' (12.32).

Conclusion

This chapter has been written in the conviction that there is far more to John's Gospel than first meets the eye. It is a piece of writing that, to put it in non-religious language, is one of extraordinary depth and power. Its language, imagery and narratives are multidimensional: their resonances and meaning are not easily exhausted. But it helps to dig a little beneath the surface. We shall return to the Gospel's story in Chapter 4, but in the next chapter we need to face some of the difficult questions raised in recent years about this Gospel.

3

Current Questions
about John's Gospel

This is a necessary chapter, if I am to carry most, if not all, my readers with me. No one can deny that the Gospel asserts that God loved the world (3.16). What many may doubt is whether John's Gospel may be called 'attractive' (see above, p.2).

I have called it attractive because its leading theme is how humankind may find light and life (1.5; 20.30–31). That is its chief appeal, but there is more. The Gospel promises not only food and drink that will satisfy humankind's hunger and quench their thirst for ever (for example 6.35); it promises even victory over death (for example 11.25). It is the Gospel that contains the words of comfort heard at funeral services: 'Let not your hearts be troubled . . .' (14.1).

Many people today, however, find John's Gospel a problem. It seems a very other-worldly Gospel in an age that looks for 'relevance'; it is alleged to portray Christians as 'in this world, but not of it' – though, as I shall try to show, this represents a serious misunderstanding. John is also thought to teach an exclusive, narrow view of other faiths: 'no one comes to the Father except by me' (John 14.6). Again, I shall argue that this is to misunderstand the Gospel.

These are not all the charges that John has faced, particularly recently. The masculine imagery that the Gospel uses of God ('Father' and 'Son') is bound to jar with those Christians who prefer 'Creator, Redeemer and Sanctifier' to 'Father, Son and Holy Spirit' in the benediction at the end of a service. There is also a wider question about the place of women in the gospel story – and, therefore, the Church. Most serious of all, this Gospel has been described as anti-Semitic, because of its many negative references to 'the Jews'.

These misunderstandings, in my view, have wrongly diminished the Gospel's genuine attractiveness. The four sections of this chapter will seek to address them.

A worldly or an other-worldly Gospel?

The problem can be quickly stated. 'The world' came to have very negative connotations in Christian history, and John's Gospel is partly, if not largely, responsible. A brief sketch of what the Gospel teaches about the *kosmos* (John's word for 'the world'), will show why this is so.

'The world' in John and Christian history

As usual, the prologue, 1.1–18, gives us the basic view: the world is God's creation, but tragically did not and does not recognize him as the source of its life and light. But still God loves the world (3.16) and works ceaselessly for it to come to faith (17.21, 23). So not all John's references to the world are negative: the Son of Man will give himself for the life of the world (6.51), he is its light (8.12; compare 9.5, 12.46), and his mission to the world is a positive one: 'I came not to judge the world, but to save the world' (12.47).

But the perspective changes in the second half of the Gospel. The last discourses of Jesus, and his prayer in the garden (chapters 14–17) are peppered with negative references to the world, although the fundamental hope of bringing the world to faith (John 17.21, 23) remains. But the world as it is *cannot* receive the gift of the Spirit, leading to life and truth (14.17); the peace Jesus gives his followers is 'not as the world gives' (14.27). Sharpest of all are the references to the world's hatred of the disciples, of Jesus, and of God (15.18–25). There is more in the same vein in chapters 16 and 17. So in this Gospel the word *kosmos* begins with a neutral meaning, but acquires increasingly negative connotations: the world *cannot* believe without ceasing to be 'the world'.

But now we need to look at what has happened in recent centuries, at least in the English-speaking world. We begin with the 1611 Authorized Version of the Bible. Its overliteral translation of some of the key phrases in John's Gospel has been enormously influential, in particular, its rendering of *ouk ek tou kosmou* as 'not of the world' (for example 17.16). The AV's influence (if not the wider, more longstanding influence of John's Gospel over the centuries), has shaped other key Christian texts. So the Book of Common Prayer asks that Christians may be delivered from 'the world, the flesh and the devil', and Bunyan's *Pilgrim's Progress* begins: 'As I walked through *the wilderness of this world*, I lighted on a certain place' (my italics). This is the background to the longstanding view that Christians are called to be 'in the world, but not of it'. Liturgical expressions such as 'Go into the world' at the end of a church service may encourage the picture of a church somehow detached from the world. It's as if 'Church' and 'world' are two adjacent circles, rather than two concentric ones.

Other influences, particularly in the early centuries, shaped the way Christians read John's Gospel. Under the Roman Empire, they often faced acute moral dilemmas and, until the end of the second century, condemned and refused military service in the Roman army. Attitudes were to change later on, but the growing influence of monasticism encouraged the idea that a person was more likely to be a better Christian if they were less, rather than more, engaged with the world. In any case, life expectancy until quite recently – and still in many parts of the world – was so short that people's thoughts were more readily directed to life in the next world, rather than to the transformation of this one.

'In the world, but not of it'? The problem

So how are Christians supposed to relate to the world according to John's Gospel? At first sight, the description of Christians as 'in the world, but not of it' seems to be exactly what this Gospel *does* say. (Paul says something similar: 'Do not be conformed to this world' (Romans 12.2).) So why is this description so misleading? We begin with John 17, because this chapter seems to confirm this traditional picture of Jesus' followers: 'And now I am no longer in the world, but they are in the world, and I am coming to you' (v. 11)', and 'they do not belong to the world [literally 'not of the world'], as I do not belong to the world' (v. 16). But is this the whole picture? The comparison with Jesus in both verses is crucial. Jesus is the model, or trailblazer for the disciples; they are in the world, as he was; they do not belong to the world, as he did not. But to understand these phrases properly, we need to go back to John's prologue, which makes it quite clear: Jesus was not 'of this world', but was sent into it. The same is true of the disciples: disciples, like 'the Word' ('the Son'), are not of this world, but are sent into it.

Isn't this the same as being 'in the world, but not of it'? Haven't we simply changed the sentence round? The reader at this point may have a sneaking suspicion I am simply playing with words. In fact, changing the sentence round makes a huge difference to how we understand both phrases: 'not of the world' and 'in the world'.

Some examples, modern and biblical, may help. People who have emigrated or been exiled from their own country may well have divided loyalties. That was the situation of the exiles to whom the prophet Jeremiah sent a letter of advice and encouragement (Jeremiah 29.5–7); they were in Babylon, but not of it, because their origins, their loyalty, their hearts lay elsewhere. Even so, Jeremiah urged the Jewish exiles to 'seek the welfare' of Babylon. Similarly, in the New Testament, Christians were in Rome, but not of it, and yet should still pay their taxes (Romans 13.7), and pray for their political rulers (1 Timothy 2.1–2).

Down the centuries this has been the traditional picture of Christians: exiles in an alien land, 'pilgrims through this barren land'. It has an important element of truth. Like the Jewish exiles in Babylon, the deepest loyalty of Christians is given, not to the world or anything in it, but to God. But the trouble with this traditional description, 'in the world, but not of it', is that it conveys a picture of a semi-detached existence. It gives a negative feel to both halves of the description: Christians have to be in this world, but would rather be elsewhere, and their commitment to it is limited because they are 'not of the world'.

The traditional picture is appropriate in some situations. Christians who are 'in the world, but not of it' might be described as living 'in survival mode'. That is how it feels in countries with governments hostile to Christian faith, where opportunities for evangelism and for social and political engagement are very limited. But is this the whole picture? And is this way of picturing Christian existence in the world appropriate in all circumstances, even when the government of the day is not a threat to the Church?

'As the Father sent me': another model of Christian existence

Let's look again at John 17. I have been suggesting that if we take seriously Jesus as the role model for the disciples, and the Gospel's prologue as our guide, we have to reverse the sentence: Jesus was not of this world, and 'the Father' sent him into it. Can this be said of the disciples? The parallels between them and Jesus are not exact, of course. The Word is God's only begotten Son (1.18), whereas the disciples were already in the world before they were sent into it (20.23). And that is just as true of Christians today, of course. Unlike Jesus, our mission to the world did not begin at birth.

But when we say Peter, Andrew and the other disciples were in the world – as obviously they were – we are talking of what we might call the old order; now there is a 'new creation'. The disciple is 'born of God' or born 'from above' (1.13; 3.3, 7)[1] through the Spirit who would be given after the resurrection (3.5–6; 7.39; 20.22–23). This rebirth through the Spirit leads to a mission: 'As the Father sent me, so I send you' (20.23).

---

1 The Greek word *anothen* (John 3.3, 7) can mean either 'from above' or 'again'; the writer was almost certainly conscious of both meanings.

So in John's Gospel, the overall sequence is clear: disciples are chosen 'out of the world', 'reborn' through the gift of the Spirit, *and then sent into the world*. In that respect, their mission is modelled on Jesus, who was sent because 'God so loved the world' (3.16).

So the model of Christian existence in the world in John's Gospel turns out to be the reverse of what we have usually thought: *not* 'in the world, but not of it', but something altogether more mission-centred: *'not of this world, but sent into it'*. John's Gospel, in fact, anticipates what the Quaker, William Penn, was to say in 1682: 'True godliness does not turn people out of the world, but enables them to live better in it and excites their endeavours to mend it.'[2] The life of the American monk, Thomas Merton, provides a powerful example. Merton entered the Abbey of Gethsemani in Kentucky as a young man in 1941. His attitude to the world he thought he was leaving behind was narrow and critical. But over the years, Merton's deepening spiritual life transformed his attitude to 'the world', and strengthened his commitment to it. For example, he was an influential critic of America's Vietnam War, and his was one of the first voices to sound the alarm about the developing ecological crisis.

If 'abiding in the Father and the Son' through the Spirit of truth (to use John's language) takes us, paradoxically, closer to the world, what are we to say of the traditional way of describing the life of Christians, 'in the world, but not of it'? First, as I have already suggested, in situations of persecution and oppression this may well be how Christian existence looks and feels: Christian living 'in survival mode' (Hebrews, 1 Peter and Revelation are examples in the New Testament). But, second, it is a one-sided picture, easily misunderstood by Christians, and by anyone else who hears this said of Christians. After all, the sentence 'he lives in Britain, but is not of it,' though odd English, would naturally be taken to mean that such a person is not as committed to Britain as other people. So Christian existence in

---

2 Jonathan Dean, *Servitude and Freedom: Reading the Christian Tradition*, London: Epworth, 2009, p. 131.

the world comes to be seen as less wholehearted and committed than that of others.

On loving the world – as God does

We should be in no doubt that important practical consequences follow from this argument. It is a mistake to think of the incarnation as an isolated incident in the life of an otherwise uninvolved God. If we think God is disengaged, we are likely to be disengaged as well.[3] If the Church misreads what John's Gospel says about 'the world', and the disciples' relationship to it, it is likely to adopt a semi-detached attitude to the wider world, at best using its mission to ensure its own survival, at worst, keeping as aloof as possible from the world's moral pollution. The negative meaning of 'the world' in John can lead us to avoid serious engagement with it altogether. Politics, for example, tends to be regarded as a dirty business; the less we have to do with it the better.

A well-known aphorism of the poet Samuel Coleridge runs as follows: 'He who begins by loving Christianity better than truth, will proceed by loving his own sect or church better than Christianity, and end in loving himself better than all.'[4] In the light of our discussion of what John's Gospel really teaches about disciples and the world, I offer an adaptation of Coleridge's words: 'They who begin by loving the Church more than the world will proceed by loving their own sect or church better than the Church (universal), and end in loving themselves better than all'.

For God so loved *the world*, and it led him in the direction of a cross.

The place of women in John's Gospel

There is another potential criticism of this Gospel that we must face. The Gospel may seem to many, especially female readers,

---

3 Daniel W. Hardy's *God's Ways with the World*, Edinburgh: T. & T. Clark, 1996, argues cogently along these lines.

4 Hardy, *God's Ways*, p. 174.

too masculine in at least three ways. It was written by a man; the range of characters is predominantly male, and perhaps most difficult of all, the language applied to God is overwhelmingly male ('Father' and 'Son').

All these points can be levelled at most of the books in the Bible. They were written by men, most of the leading characters are men, and the God of the Bible is often described as male. None of these charges can be rebutted. The question is how we interpret such a Bible, and what kind of faith and practice grow out of it.

The writer of John's Gospel is likely to have been male. Whoever 'the disciple whom Jesus loved' was, the only candidates proposed for this role have been men; if not John the son of Zebedee, then perhaps Nathaniel or Lazarus. Similarly, it is hardly surprising that most of the dramatis personae in the pages of this Gospel are men; Jesus chose twelve men to be his disciples.

Jesus' equality of regard

What was the attitude of Jesus to women? There is a danger of reading too much into the Gospels; there is insufficient evidence to show that Jesus' attitude to women was revolutionary, and radically different from that of his contemporaries. What can, I think, be shown is that Jesus seems to have shown 'equality of regard' – not just to women, but to children, to society's marginalized and, even if not at first, to Gentiles as well. 'What Jesus indicated by his practice . . . is that we are all of equal value in the eyes of God.'[5]

John's Gospel reflects something of this 'equality of regard'. Whatever the historical content of the story of Jesus' encounter with the woman of Samaria, and its undoubted symbolism, it is of a piece with stories in the other Gospels of Jesus' meetings with women: 'They [the disciples] were astonished that he was speaking with a woman' (John 4.27).

---

5 I owe the phrase 'equality of regard' in this context to David Brown's *Discipleship and Imagination. Christian Tradition and Truth*, Oxford: Oxford University Press, 2000, pp. 18ff.

This isn't the only story in John's Gospel featuring a woman. The mother of Jesus appears at the beginning of Jesus' ministry (2.1) and, with other women, at the end of his life (19.25–27); there is the story of the woman taken in adultery (7.53–8.11), missing from many of the oldest manuscripts of John's Gospel and so, perhaps, a later addition; chapter 11 prominently features Martha and Mary, who otherwise appear in the four Gospels only in Luke (10.38–42); Mary reappears in John 12.1–8 and, finally, Mary Magdalene, who had been present at the crucifixion (19.25), is the first visitor to the empty tomb, and the first person to whom the risen Jesus appears (20.1–18).[6] Two of these stories deserve particular attention in any discussion about the place of women in John's Gospel.

The testimony of Martha

This may seem to be very little, compared with the prominence of men in the Gospel story. But, few though the women are in John, their stories contain some remarkable features. In the story of the raising of Lazarus we have the testimony of Martha: 'She said to him, "Yes, Lord, I believe that you are the Messiah [in Greek, '*the Christ*'], the Son of God, the one coming into the world"' (11.27). This is the fullest expression of faith that anyone has yet made in this Gospel. It exceeds Nathaniel's 'Rabbi, you are the Son of God! You are the King of Israel!' (1.49); in a sense, it surpasses that of the Samaritans, 'we know that this is truly the Saviour of the world' (4.42), and it exceeds the faith implied in the once-blind man, model disciple though he may be (9.35–38). Here, by what she says, Martha fulfils explicitly the stated purpose of the Gospel. She is the first character to confess her faith in Jesus as 'the Christ, the Son of God' (compare 20.30–31). Her testimony of faith is all the more significant, coming as it

---

6 Space precludes a detailed study of the story of the anointing of Jesus (12.1–8). It is only John who identifies the woman in this story as Mary. The other versions in Mark and Matthew are very like each other (Mark 14.3–9; Matthew 26.6–13), and more like John's anointing story than that of Luke (Luke 7.36–50). Given these variations, we cannot now prove – or disprove – that the woman in the original event was Mary.

does at the heart of the dramatic account of the greatest sign of all the signs recounted in John's Gospel.

Mary Magdalene and the risen Christ

The other passage which deserves our attention here is the resurrection story which features – far more prominently than the other Gospels – Mary Magdalene. Scholars have long pondered the differences between what the Gospels, or some of them, say about the appearances of the risen Christ, and what Paul says. According to Matthew some women saw the risen Jesus first (Matthew 28.9); John mentions only Mary Magdalene, whereas, according to Paul, the risen Christ first appeared to 'Cephas' – that is Peter (1 Corinthians 15.3–8). Paul makes no mention of the women. It is sometimes said that he omits them because the testimony of women did not count in those days. I am not so sure about that. They are more likely to have been left out of Paul's list – and it was a list passed on to him (1 Corinthians 15.3) – not because they were women, but because they were not apostles. So we have to take seriously the tradition that it was Peter to whom Jesus appeared first, while recognizing that John seems to know, and chooses to say, that it was Mary to whom Jesus first came. That, in itself, is enormously important in gauging the place of women in his Gospel.

Three features stand out in this story of Mary at the tomb. First, Mary weeps, and the last person to weep in this Gospel was Jesus himself (11.35), and that also was outside a tomb. Then, however, there was a body inside the tomb – that of Lazarus – and Jesus shed his tears along with Mary and the Jews who accompanied her (11.33). Did the writer recall what he had written earlier about the tears of Jesus? Probably he did. So the references to weeping are a striking example of what the Church came to believe about him: he lived our life, shed our tears, and died our death so that, as the last book of the Bible promises, 'every tear' will be wiped away (Revelation 21.4). Here, as in most things about Jesus, what matters is his humanity, not his maleness.

There is another detail which connects with what the Gospel has said earlier about the good shepherd: 'he will call his sheep by name . . . and the sheep follow him because they know his voice' (10.3–4). In the resurrection story that is precisely what happens. The first 'sheep' to be called by name is a woman: 'Jesus said to her "Mary!" She turned and said to him in Hebrew "Rabbouni!"' (20.16).

But the climax of the story has yet to come. It has often been noticed that, of all the New Testament writers, only Luke recounts the resurrection and ascension of Jesus as two separate events. Here John makes no such distinction. As he has done throughout the second half of his Gospel, he underscores yet again the return of Jesus to the Father:

> Jesus said to her, 'Do not hold on to me, because I have not yet ascended to the Father. But go to my brothers and say to them, "I *am ascending* to my Father and your Father, my God and your God."' (20. 17)

It is no coincidence that this is the first time in this Gospel that Jesus refers to God, not just as 'my Father' and 'my God', but as 'your Father' and 'your God'. That is the difference which his coming from heaven and returning to heaven has made. Did this mean that before the coming of Jesus no one could, or did, address God as 'my Father'? In the literal sense, that was patently not so. But now something new has happened. This Gospel claims, in different ways, that 'the Word made flesh' – Jesus coming from and returning to God – has made a 'bridge' which was not there before. (Jesus' words to Nathaniel implicitly comparing himself as the Son of Man to Jacob's ladder, is one such expression of this claim (1.51).)

So this story ends with Mary Magdalene's testimony, 'I have seen the Lord' (20.18). She is the first person to say that, and it is significant that the evangelist has chosen a woman as the first privileged recipient of a resurrection appearance. By that I do not mean that he has made it up, but that he is likely to have known the tradition that Peter was the first to see the risen Jesus (1 Corinthians 15.3), and that he could have 'led' with that story by passing over the tradition that women, or a woman, saw Jesus first.

This story, along with the others in the Gospel, which we have noted in this section, amply illustrates John's equality of regard for women. But it is not enough to say this. The paramount question for us, as always, is what kind of faith and practice emerge out of our reading of the Bible.

The hardest question, in my view, still remains to be tackled, namely the preponderance of male imagery applied to God, particularly Father–Son language. Many who read this book will have noticed the tendency in church services, in recent decades, to substitute the traditional words of the benediction, Father, Son and Spirit, with words such as 'Creator, Redeemer and Sanctifier'. At the same time, the use of 'Mother' as a form of address to God continues to be controversial. These contemporary controversies make it all the more important to address the question of the language for God used in John's Gospel.

Two fundamental reference points must guide our discussion. First, the central Christian doctrine about God is the Trinity, and it is a fact of early Christian history that John's Gospel made a massive contribution to the development of that doctrine. That cannot change, without Christianity becoming, in effect, another religion. I might add here that the trouble with substitutes for the traditional language of Father, Son and Holy Spirit – such as 'Creator, Redeemer and Sanctifier' – is that they describe three functions of God; they say nothing about the relationships of the three persons of the Trinity. This is not to say that they are wrong but that, in this respect at least, they are inadequate, and should not become a permanent substitute for the traditional form.

The second key point in our discussion is the nature of all our language about God. It can only ever be approximate. We are seeking to use mere words about a mystery that transcends all our words and ideas. And that must be true of even the language which Jesus used. To say otherwise is, in effect, to deny that he was really human and subject to the limitations of a human language like the rest of us. So it must follow that, while Jesus' own language about God has a special place in Christian tradition, we can't enshrine it in an eternal typeset as if it were not, after all, human language which we are talking about. We should not make idols of even the most precious and valued images we use about God.

So where does this leave us in our discussion about the Gospel of John? Of course, the word 'Son' applied to Jesus reinforces the point that it is a masculine image; Jesus, after all, was a man. But he was called 'Son of God' for reasons which had nothing to do with his gender. He came from God, he was like God, and he fulfilled the hopes and aspirations of Israel about a future deliverer. So the background and use of the title 'Son of God' points beyond mere gender.

In any case, this Gospel is noteworthy for the number of times it uses the word 'human being' (*anthropos*) of Jesus, the words of Pilate (19.5) being particularly striking: 'See, the human being!' By contrast, the word 'man' (*aner*, as opposed to 'woman,' *gyne*) is used of Jesus only once (1.30), and infrequently elsewhere in the New Testament (Acts 17.31 is a rare example). Given the background, the culture and the history into which Jesus was born, it is well-nigh impossible to imagine God sending, not a son, but a daughter. Yet we can perhaps just imagine that, in another culture with a different history, if the situation had required it, God would have become incarnate as a woman, on the incarnational principle that God will do whatever it takes to save the world.

But now we must turn to the other word central to our discussion: 'Father'. It is easy to suppose that this word, too, is inescapably and irretrievably masculine. Understood literally, of course, it is. But like the word 'Son', the word 'Father', applied to God, also transcends gender. We might well ask: how could it be otherwise? But we still have to ask what it means. Two general points are perhaps worth making. First, I suggest that God was called 'Father' not just because biblical cultures were patriarchal – which they were – and still less because God is male, but because God loves in a parent-like way. The second point is this: the Gospel of John – and Paul – shows that the word 'Father' applied to God is an eschatological word: that is, it belongs to God's new creation. We receive the privilege of calling God 'Father' when we are baptized into a new life or, in John's language, we are born again (Galatians 4.6 and Romans 8.15 are two clear examples in the writings of Paul). As we have noticed, Jesus first refers to his Father as the Father also of the disciples after the resurrection, but not before.

Because God is not literally anyone's Father (because God is spirit, not physical), we have to say that the word 'Father' applied to God is a metaphor. The trouble is that this particular metaphor has lost its freshness, and we need to recover, if we can, what was fresh and transforming about Jesus' use of this word. Transforming it would have been, since a metaphor, if it is to be an effective metaphor, helps those who hear it to see the person or object differently from before. From beginning to end, the Gospel makes very clear that we can only understand what is meant by 'Father' applied to God by looking at the Son: 'Whoever has seen me has seen the Father' (14.9). 'Father' and 'Son', applied to God, are metaphors – and both metaphors, precisely because that is what they are, point beyond gender.

It is time to summarize, and to make a few practical points. We should not deny the central importance of the Trinity in the Christian understanding of God. At the same time, we should not make an idol of even the most hallowed terms: all words used about God are approximations to a truth and a mystery beyond words. So we need to see how both words, Father and Son, transcend gender. The God revealed in Jesus invites all – women and men alike – into a new life and a new community where there is equality of regard.

That doesn't solve everything, as those women know who have experienced gender injustice at the hands of Christian men behaving badly, sometimes men holding high office in the Church. It is harder to appreciate the theological and linguistic arguments I have been putting forward here if all you can see around you in the Church is gender injustice and sexual discrimination. But I hope the time will come soon when such injustice will no longer be an impediment to receiving the imagery of John's Gospel in the way I have described.

This argument doesn't solve all our problems about the language we use of God. Which pronoun should we use – 'he', 'she' or 'it'? None is exactly right, since God is neither male nor female nor neuter. It may be best, as David Ford suggests, to use 'he' on the grounds that it draws less attention to itself.[7] But he goes on to say that 'I' and 'You' are much nearer the heart of the matter, because whether we speak or are silent about God, we are never out of his presence, the One whom a seminal revelation in the Bible calls 'I am'.[8]

We live in unsettled times, and so all our experimenting with language may be quite healthy, especially if it reminds that, at the end of the day, all our words and images of God are inadequate. It seems appropriate to end this section with the testimony of Mother Julian of Norwich, who certainly didn't feel tied to biblical language, even though her language has its roots in the Bible:

> In this way I saw that God was rejoicing to be our Father; rejoicing too to be our Mother; and rejoicing yet again to be our true Husband, with our soul his beloved wife. And Christ rejoices to be our Brother, and our Saviour too. These five great joys I believe he intends us to enjoy too – praising, thanking, loving, blessing him for ever.[9]

Even more remarkable is Julian's description of Christ as 'our Mother': Jesus Christ who sets good against evil is 'our real Mother'.[10]

John's Gospel and other faiths: how exclusive is John's Gospel?

As in the first two sections of this chapter, I should like to carry my readers with me in the argument that follows. So let me make

---

7 David F. Ford, *The Shape of Living*, Grand Rapids: Zondervan, 1997, pp. 182–3.

8 Isaiah 64.8 addresses God as 'our Father', and Wisdom 2.16, in its portrait of the just man, envisages him boasting of God as his father. There are other examples, in the Old Testament and in later Jewish writings, but it is still true to say that 'Father' as a term for God acquires a centrality in Christian writings it had not had before.

9 Julian of Norwich, *Revelations of Divine Love*, translated into modern English by Clifton Wolters, Harmondsworth: Penguin Classics, 1966, chp. 52, p. 151. See also chps 58 and 59 for other examples of God as Mother in Julian's writings.

10 Examples occur in *Revelations* chps 58 and 59.

clear what I am *not* doing. I am *not* arguing that all faiths are basically the same in the end, and so it doesn't matter if you are a Christian or a Muslim, so long as you are sincere. Nor am I denying what I take to be the central Christian conviction about God: that he is eternally Father, Son and Holy Spirit. Such a conviction grew, however gradually and even tortuously, I believe, from the conviction expressed in this Gospel's prologue: the Word was made flesh. What I am seeking to show is that Christians are mistaken in applying to the question of other faiths a verse often quoted from this Gospel: 'Jesus said to him [Thomas], "I am the way, and the truth and the life. No one comes to the Father except through me"' (14.6).

The first step, as always, in trying to understand a verse from the Bible, is to notice what the words are. We very easily paraphrase this verse in our minds, and imagine it is saying, 'No one comes to the Father, *unless they believe in me*', or 'No one comes to the Father *unless they become a Christian*'. But if that is not the meaning of the verse, what does it mean? We need to take our next step, which is to look more closely at the original context of the verse.

Every verse in the Bible has two contexts: a literary one and a historical one. In exploring the literary context, we are asking questions such as these: Do the preceding and following verses shed light on the verse we are studying? and Does the rest of the Gospel shed any light on this verse? In looking at the historical context, we are asking questions such as: When were these words first spoken or written down? and Can we see what the author intended by them? So looking at a text in its different contexts is rather like looking at a painting from different angles, or holding up a precious jewel to the light, and turning it now this way, now that.

The historical origins of John 14.6

To take the historical context first: it is reasonable to suppose that these words originated in some form or other with Jesus himself. As we have seen in Chapter 2, it is possible sometimes to see behind a saying of Jesus in John a saying in one of the other Gospels which may well be a more original version of it. In this case, there is a saying, occurring in identical form in Matthew's and Luke's Gospels, from which John 14.6 may derive:

'All things have been handed over to me by my Father; and no one knows the Son except the Father, and no one knows the Father except the Son and anyone to whom the Son chooses to reveal him.' (Matthew 11.27; Luke 10.22)

Here are two affirmations, one of which is very like the claim of John 14.6: 'No one knows the Father except the Son and anyone to whom the Son chooses to reveal him' (compare 'no one comes to the Father except through me'). So the revelation of both the Father and the Son is *one* revelation: it is impossible that the Father should be revealed without the Son, and vice versa.[11] This seems to be the nub of our problem of exclusiveness, and we shall need to return to this. But in the version in Matthew and Luke there is an emphasis different from our normal interpretation of John 14.6. We tend to place the emphasis on human response and choice: no one comes to the Father unless they (decide to) believe in Jesus. The New Testament looks at this differently, especially John's Gospel: no one becomes a Christian unless the Father draws them (for example John 6.44, 65).

This is an unfashionable, difficult idea in many modern cultures, with their emphasis on human initiative and decision. We seem to be exchanging one difficulty for another, ending up being as exclusive as ever: only those whom God chooses become Christians, and so no one comes to the Father unless God, through his Son, enables them to do so. But, uncongenial though this idea is in cultures intoxicated by choice, we need to keep it firmly in mind. It may be an important corrective to our very human-centred ideas of the Christian life.

There is another possible dimension to the original historical context of John 14.6, and that's to be found in the First Epistle of John. The Gospel and Epistles of John present us with a chicken-and-egg

---

11 See, for example, N. Richardson, *God in the New Testament*, Peterborough: Epworth, 1999, pp. 19–20.

question. They carry the same name, and the language of the Gospel and Epistles, while sounding different from other New Testament writings, has a marked similarity. So which came first? That's not a straightforward question. We have taken the view that the Gospel took shape gradually – perhaps over several decades (on this see Chapter 2). So it is quite likely that the Gospel evolved before, during and after the writing of the Epistles. So the problems highlighted in the Epistles, especially 1 John, are also reflected in the Gospel. 1 John 2.22–23 seems very close to John 14.6: 'Who is the liar but the one who denies that Jesus is the Christ? This is the antichrist, the one who denies the Father and the Son. No one who denies the Son has the Father, everyone who confesses the Son has the Father also.'

Once again, we seem to be compounding the problem: these verses sound intolerant and exclusive. But we need to note, first, that they are directed against another group claiming to be Christian, not against people of another faith. So what was at stake here, at least from the viewpoint of the writer, was the core belief of the Church: what the Church later came to call the humanity and divinity of Jesus.

So, to summarize this stage of the argument: whether the words come originally from Jesus himself, or whether they derive from John's own church community, they were not addressing the issue of other religions. The historical context of John 14.6 does not seem to be related to arguments with people of other faiths at all. If the situation reflected in 1 John influenced the way in which the author of the Gospel worded this saying of Jesus, then it was directed against what he believed was a deeply mistaken view of Jesus held by a rival group of Christians.

So much for the possible historical origins of this verse, and the way in which it has been worded in John's Gospel. What of the literary context of this verse? Can the preceding and following verses shed any light on its meaning?

A promise, not a threat?

The first thing to observe is that, while we often make this verse a forbidding, exclusive-sounding verse (wagging our finger at people of other faiths or, as far as we can tell, of no faith), the original context is very positive. The preceding and following verses are full of promises (13.36; 14.2–3, 7). For example: 'In my Father's house there are many dwelling-places . . . And if I go to prepare a place for you, I will come again and will take you to myself, so that where I am, there you may be also' (14.2–3).

Unfortunately, this last verse has often been translated in a way what makes it sound more negative than it should be. The NRSV has probably got it right in translating: 'If you know me, you will know my Father also. From now on you do know him and have seen him.'

The Father/Son sayings in Matthew and Luke which we noted earlier are also set in positive contexts; they tell of liberation from burdens (Matthew), and of unprecedented joy (Luke). So John 14.6 needs to be heard differently. Knowledge of the Father and the Son go together, and people don't make themselves Christians; it is God through his Son who does that. This is a very different emphasis from our usual understanding of God 'nodding through' only those who have made the right choice – that is for Christ.

But now we must ask whether this work of grace is something revealed and enhanced by Jesus, or restricted to him.

John's Gospel and other faiths

Christians came to believe that Jesus was the incarnation of God's eternal Son. John's Gospel is the New Testament writing which, more than any other, expounds this theme. John makes the important connection: the Son is the eternal Word. So Jesus was not God's first word but, rather, God's fullest and most definitive word. But that word existed in the world before the coming of Jesus; this is the likeliest meaning of John 1.10: 'He was in the world, and the world came into being through him; yet the world did not know him.'

Other verses in the New Testament point the same way. Christ was present in the wilderness, refreshing and sustaining the children of Israel (1 Corinthians 10.4). Moses, long before the coming of Jesus, shared 'the reproach of Christ' (Hebrews 11.26). Language like this has wider implications. One of the greatest nineteenth-century students of John's Gospel, Bishop Westcott, had this to say about the eternal Word: 'From the first He was (so to speak) on his way to the world, advancing toward the Incarnation by preparatory revelations.' So the eternal Word, says Westcott, which enlightens all people, may be called 'the spiritual Sun'. This understanding of the opening verses of John's Gospel leads him to say this about John 14.6: 'It is only through Christ that we can . . . apprehend God as the Father, and so approach the Father . . . It does not follow that everyone who is guided by Christ is directly conscious of His guidance.'[12]

Some readers may hesitate about this understanding of John's Gospel: does it compromise the uniqueness of Jesus? Are we doing justice to John's Gospel? And isn't there still an exclusive dimension of this Gospel? I shall address these three questions in turn.

The uniqueness of Jesus and the Gospel of John

If pressed, I should want firmly to insist: no, we do not compromise the uniqueness of Jesus, reducing him to the status of one prophet or saviour among several. But there are good reasons for avoiding the words 'unique' and 'uniqueness'. They are not words that need to be used in evangelizing in a multi-faith world. The word 'unique' easily becomes a triumphalist Christian slogan and few, if any of us, know enough about other faiths to win the argument. But the very word 'win' expresses the dubious nature of the whole enterprise. There are better ways of witnessing to Jesus than arguing for his uniqueness. But, in case my protest about using the word 'unique' about Jesus be thought to dodge the issue, I still want to maintain, as long as the doctrines of the incarnation and trinity remain, as I think they must, the heart of Christian faith, then the 'uniqueness' of Jesus is safeguarded.

---

12 Graham A. Patrick, *The Miner's Bishop. Brooke Foss Westcott*, Peterborough: Epworth, 2004, p. 169.

Our second question was: does the interpretation we are offering here do justice to John's Gospel? So far we have concentrated on the opening verses of the Gospel and John 14.6. But it is clear that the cross and resurrection of Jesus are quite central to an understanding of his person and his work. The evangelist leaves us in no doubt, as the story unfolds, that the cross and resurrection are an unprecedented fulfilment, revelation, experience – all these words are appropriate. So much of John's language points in that direction: 'the hour' (not just any hour) is the revelation of God's love *eis telos* (13.1); the glorifying of the Father and the Son (13.31–32), and the lifting up of the Son of Man which will bring life to the world (3.14; 12.32) are the climax of that revelation. All this language, if we are to do justice to John's Gospel, must be set in the framework of God's eternal, universal love.

An exclusive Gospel?

Finally, is there still an exclusive dimension in this Gospel, and particularly in John 14.6: 'no one comes to the Father except by me'? I think there was, and there is. In its original context, this verse might well have been heard as excluding 'the Jews', and the Jews themselves would have found this Gospel difficult, to put it mildly (see below). Earlier chapters, especially chapters 8, 9 and 10, challenged some fundamental Jewish beliefs: that they knew God (8.19), that they were free (8.33), that they were children of Abraham (8.39), and that God was their Father (8.41–44). This Gospel insists from start to finish that knowledge of Father and Son belong inseparably together.

Does this not mean we end up where we started, excluding people of other faiths? Not necessarily. We need to notice three things. First, according to the New Testament, there were devout Jews who welcomed Jesus with open arms: Simeon and Anna (Luke 2.25–38), and Joseph of Arimethea (Mark 15.43). Such characters are portrayed almost as Christians before Christ. More importantly, those who rejected Jesus are shown as ignoring the direction in which their own faith was pointing. If they had really paid heed to Moses and the Scriptures, they would have welcomed Jesus and followed his way (for example John 5.39, 46; Luke 16.31).

This picture of Jews who, by their alleged unfaithfulness to their Scriptures and traditions, were blind to the reality and identity of Jesus, applies to 'Christians' too. For example, when a churchgoer puts a moribund tradition or a moribund building before the claims of the Gospel, or of charity, is this not the equivalent of rejecting Jesus? On this understanding, John 14.6 excludes some 'Christians' as well.

And that brings us back to the original context of John's Gospel. We know from 1 John that there were so-called Christians who seem to have imagined that they had access to the Father despite bypassing the Son; they rejected the cross and, in the process, rejected the claims of love as well (for example 1 John 2.23; 3.14–18).

What of today? If some people in John's day were seen to be excluded from the way to God, will that not also be true today? That may be so. But it is not for us to draw the lines. And it is not for us to wrench John 14.6 (and similar verses) from its original context of promise and hope for disciples, and to use it in a quite different way as a weapon against people of other faiths or of no faith. To do so is hardly the best way to evangelize, nor a proper use of John's Gospel.

I end this section with the testimony of a remarkable Christian – a student of Bishop Westcott – who served the Church in India. C. F. Andrews went out to Delhi in 1904 and was quickly involved in dialogues with scholars of other faiths. He became estranged from his own church, even repudiating his priestly orders. But two of the most famous people in India at this time were deeply impressed by Andrews. The Hindu scholar and poet Rabindranath Tagore wrote of him that 'nowhere had he seen "such a triumph of Christianity"', and Gandhi called him 'the pattern of the ideal missionary' and even 'love incarnate'. It would be a mistake to think that C. F. Andrews drifted away from orthodox Christianity. After nearly 30 years in India he wrote: 'Christ has become not less central but more central; not less divine to me, but more so, because more universally human. I can see Him as the pattern of all that is best in Asia as well as in Europe.'[13] The light is universal: 'the true light which enlightens everyone, was coming into the world'. Yet the light has become an enfleshed Word: 'And the Word became flesh and dwelt among us, and we have seen his glory, the glory as of a father's only son, full of grace and truth' (1.9, 14). Because that Word is universal in its presence, fully revealed in Jesus, and because that Word is God, it must, for the Christian, be a matter of fact that no one comes to the eternal Father except by the eternal Son. If the Father and Son are undivided, how could it be otherwise?

Is John anti-Semitic?

I have reserved until last what I believe is the hardest question of all. Readers to whom this is a new question may be shocked that it could even be asked of one of the Gospel writers. (Luke, though, has also been accused of being anti-Semitic.) Other readers, however, may have been troubled by the acrimonious exchanges between Jesus and 'the Jews' in John. The very negative portrait of 'the Jews' in this Gospel requires some explanation – and, if possible, some justification. (We need to use quotation marks in order to convey the fact that it is John's language that we are talking about.) Since the Holocaust in the twentieth century, New Testament scholars have become increasingly conscious, not only of a tendency in the Church towards anti-Semitism down the centuries, but also of verses in the New Testament (Luke, Paul and John in particular) which may have contributed to this ugly feature of Christian history.

First, though, it will be useful to clarify some key terms. 'Anti-Semitism' is probably best understood as a kind of racism; the Nazis' genocide of the 1930s and 1940s was a terrible example of it. There can be no doubt that some Christians have been guilty of such racism, and continue to be. But 'anti-Semitic' needs to be distinguished from 'anti-Jewish'. To criticize Israeli foreign policy (for example) would not be anti-Semitic, unless the criticism

---

13 Patrick, *The Miner's Bishop*, pp. 165f.

was motivated by racism. So it may be better to ask whether the Gospel of John is anti-Jewish, rather than anti-Semitic. Racism has always been an ugly feature of the human scene; the ancient world was no exception. But it is unlikely to have been an ingredient of the apparent anti-Jewishness of John's Gospel, since it is likely that this Gospel grew out of a Jewish Christian community (see Chapter 2).

The problem we are addressing in this section can be quickly stated. The evangelist uses the term 'the Jews' in an undifferentiated way, as if, in their response to Jesus, the Jewish people were all the same. But that is not all. 'The Jews' might suggest the entire nation. A reference today to 'the British' or 'the Americans' would suggest that, unless the reference was in a clearly defined context such as a war in the Middle East; in that case, people would know that 'the British' meant the British soldiers fighting there.

Before we address the issue directly, it will be helpful to review at least some of the problem passages in the Gospel.

When we compare John with Mark, Matthew and Luke, we see at once some major differences. Gone from John's Gospel are 'the scribes' and 'the Sadducees', though the chief priests and the Pharisees are still there. Instead, there are well over 50 references to 'the Jews', and hardly any in the other Gospels.[14]

The frequent references to 'the Jews' in John requires some explanation. After all, why should it be used in an account of the life and ministry of Jesus, a Jew himself, when that life and ministry were spent entirely among fellow Jews, with very few encounters indeed with non-Jews?[15] It's almost as if the writer has forgotten, when he writes about the healing of the blind man, and the scepticism of 'the Jews' (9.18) that the blind man and

---

14 In Matthew, Mark and Luke the term 'the Jews' occurs almost entirely in the accounts of the trial and crucifixion of Jesus in the phrase 'the king of the Jews'.

15 Jesus meets a Gentile woman (Mark 7.24–30; Matthew 15.21–28) and heals a Roman centurion's servant (Luke 7.1–10; Matthew 8.5–13) – in Luke's version, interestingly, through Jewish intermediaries. It is not clear in John's similar story (4.46–54) whether the 'royal official' is a Gentile or not.

his parents would have been Jews as well. A similar life-story of an Englishman or woman, set in England, would not be constantly referring to 'the English', unless perhaps, the author was not English, or was writing in another country for non-English readers. That may be part of the explanation here: John was writing from a greater distance in time from the life of Jesus than Matthew, Mark or Luke. But, true though this may be, it hardly touches the surface of the problem we are facing here.

The deeper problem is not the frequency of references to 'the Jews', but the increasingly bitter tone of the exchanges between 'the Jews' and Jesus. The tone is sharpest of all in the words of Jesus in chapter 8:

'You are from your father the devil, and you choose to do your father's desires. He was a murderer from the beginning and does not stand in the truth, because there is no truth in him. When he lies he speaks according to his own nature, for he is a liar and the father of lies. But because I tell you the truth, you do not believe me'. (8.44–45)

(The context, vv. 31, 48, shows that these searing remarks are addressed to 'the Jews' who, we might note, give as good as they get (vv. 48, 52). But that, of course, is most definitely not the point.)

The American Jewish scholar Adele Reinhartz, in her book *Befriending the Beloved Disciple: A Jewish Reading of the Gospel of John*, suggests that reading a book is like befriending its author – hence the title of her book.[16] But the Beloved Disciple, she argues, offers his friendship in very 'either/or' terms to his readers: 'Accept the gift I am offering – or don't accept it; there is no neutral position.' That is certainly the nature of the story that the Beloved Disciple tells: a neutral position is not possible – you are either for or against Jesus. Unfortunately – as it seems to many – part of the evangelist's 'package' to his readers is the

---

16 A. Reinhartz, *Befriending the Beloved Disciple: A Jewish Reading of the Gospel of John*, New York: Continuum, 2001.

almost uniformly negative picture of 'the Jews' which domi-
nates not only the middle chapters of the Gospel (on these see
Chapter 4), but also the passion narrative (chapters 18 and 19).
Reinhartz calls readers who accept the author's gift 'compliant'
readers; those who don't are 'resistant' readers. Her argument
is simple. 'The Jews' in John illustrate the negative response to
the author's gift; they are portrayed as 'a violent and repugnant
people, filled with hatred and misunderstanding'.[17] So, she concludes, a compliant reader is bound to come 'perilously close to
outright hostility to Jews as a group'.

I suggest that all Christian readers of John's Gospel must take
Reinhartz' argument very seriously. Christian readers, by definition, embrace the gift which the author is offering; do we also
accept the negative picture of 'the Jews' which seems inseparable
from the gift? The undeniably 'either/or' character of this Gospel
seems to push us in the direction of being either for or against
Jesus (no neutral ground). But if we are for him, then, it seems,
we are bound to be against 'the Jews', since they epitomize the
opposition to Jesus.

What is to be said in response to this charge of apparent anti-
Jewishness in John? It is natural for most Christians to spring to
the defence of the Bible – or at least the New Testament – when
it is attacked. But a few moments' leafing through John should
be enough to confirm that there is a case to answer. And, as I
have pointed out, Christian history is deeply stained by an anti-
Semitism whose origins might well be in the New Testament itself. Even in my lifetime, I am told, Jewish children have been
subjected to abuse in school playgrounds, on the grounds that
the Jewish people were responsible for the death of Jesus.

It is difficult, if not impossible, to refute the observation of
Adele Reinhartz that the Jews in John's Gospel act as a foil for
Jesus. I pointed out in the last chapter that the story this au-
thor tells cannot be read as a straightforward historical account.
Rooted in history it undoubtedly is, with likely historical details
about Jesus not carried by the other Gospels. But it is also the

---

17 Reinhartz, *Befriending*, pp. 64, 66.

product of later reflection – by John and his community. This is the point to begin in trying to understand the role of 'the Jews', in this Gospel.

In an earlier section of this book, 'The journey of the Beloved Disciple' (Chapter 2), we speculated that John and his community may well have fled, with the onset of the Jewish Roman wars of AD 68–71, from Jerusalem to Ephesus. Such a journey may have been both traumatic and transforming. Even if John in Ephesus was no further away from Judaea than Luke, his migration may have influenced his perspective more than Luke's travels shaped his. That observation doesn't reduce the nature of the problem we are addressing here, but it may go a little way towards helping us to understand it. There are also two other points to add here. First, this particular difference between John and the other Gospels may be a striking, or problematic, example of John carrying on where the others left off. He stands back, as it were from some, though not all, historical details. He looks at Jesus' rejection by his own people from a greater distance: 'He came . . . to his own people, and his own people did not receive him.'

This verse from the prologue brings us to the second point. In this Gospel, as we have noticed, representative people do and say things which are meant to represent their 'type'; Nathaniel, 'an Israelite indeed', and Nicodemus, a Pharisee and 'teacher of Israel', are obvious examples. In John's Gospel – uncomfortable though this detail is – 'the Jews' represent 'the world' which, in the darkness of its unbelief, rejects Jesus. (The verse just quoted, as we saw in Chapter 1, could equally well describe Jesus' own Jewish people, or the entire human race.)

A quick overview of the Gospel will show that 'the Jews' do indeed seem to be a microcosm of the world – a further reason for enclosing every reference to them in quotation marks. The prologue, as always, provides a synopsis of what is to be narrated, and as we saw in Chapter 1, 'his own people' probably means, in this context (vv. 10, 11), *both* the Jewish people *and* the whole world. Subsequent chapters supply the detail. In chapters 5—12 'the Jews' act out the tragic ignorance and rejection of that Word which is the light of humankind. In

Jesus' last discourses and prayer of chapters 14–17, the world is described in words that recall the earlier chapters. The world's hatred (15.18ff.), for example, recalls the murderous atmosphere of chapter 8 (for example v. 37). Conversely, Jesus' rebuke of 'the Jews' in chapter 8 – 'you are of this world, I am not of this world' (v. 23) – anticipates the stark contrast between the world and Jesus' disciples, expressed in the prayer of chapter 17. But if 'the Jews' are a microcosm of 'the world' and Jesus and his disciples are not 'of this world', does that mean that there is a great, unbridgeable gulf between 'the Jews' and the Christian community? I shall return to this question shortly.

It is not difficult to see why this Gospel has been described as anti-Semitic; references to 'the Jews' are almost always negative, and in chapter 8, especially, the language used of them is very strong. Even if 'anti-Jewish' is a more accurate description than 'anti-Semitic', it is not difficult to see how the one easily leads to the other. How are we to respond?

Some have suggested that each time John wrote *Ioudaioi* he meant, not the Jewish people as a whole, but 'the Judaeans' – that is the people living in Judaea. It is an unlikely theory. For example, the Gospel refers to 'the Jews' in a chapter set in Galilee (chapter 6); we might well ask what 'Judaeans' from much further south were doing in Galilee. Others have argued that 'the Jews' in this Gospel refers to the Jewish leaders. That would make the expression much less ugly and difficult, but this doesn't fit the facts either. It could fit John 1.19, but breaks down on verses such as 3.1 (Nicodemus 'a leader of the Jewish leaders') and 5.1 ('a festival of the Jewish leaders').

In spite of all these very real difficulties, we can go some way towards explaining the sharpness of John's language. In the ancient world, including the Jewish world, people didn't pull their punches or mince their words in disputes with those with whom they disagreed. By our relatively polite standards, the language seems fierce and even abusive, but it was quite normal in those days. The beleaguered situation of John's community – under pressure from synagogue and empire alike – may have sharpened the community's response.

There are references in the New Testament to Jewish persecution of Christians, although 'persecution' may exaggerate what actually took place.[18] Tension and conflict there undoubtedly was, but it may have been localized and sporadic. Jewish communities may well have been exasperated by these newcomers – or renegades – so like, and yet unlike themselves. They may have been alarmed at being tarred with the same brush as the Christians by the Roman authorities. They would have been deeply offended not only by the message of a crucified Messiah (1 Corinthians 1.23), but also annoyed, if not enraged, by the way at least some Christians sat lightly to revered laws such as not eating pork.

There is another, in my view, important point to add here. In the first section of this chapter, we explored Christian attitudes to 'the world' in the light of John's teaching. I suggested that it is a mistake to picture 'the Church' and 'the world' as two quite separate entities. The Church is part of the world, whether we think of the world positively as God's creation, or negatively as a fallen creation. But if Church and world cannot be neatly separated, it follows that 'Christian' and 'Jew' cannot either. Adele Reinhartz – the Jewish scholar to whom I referred earlier – makes this very point: those who confess Jesus as Messiah and those who don't shouldn't be identified simply as 'Christian' and 'Jewish'. And it is noteworthy that those 'Jews' for whom the sharpest language is reserved (8.44–45) were 'Jews' who had believed in Jesus (8.31).

We have to be honest both about John's Gospel and about its potential effect on us. We have seen how John's language about 'the world' becomes increasingly negative – so much so that we can easily be misled into picturing 'Church' and 'world' as two adjacent circles, rather than two concentric ones. Yet God made the world, God loves the world, sending his Son, and 'the Word

---

18 Many scholars take the view that Matthew, and Luke in the Acts of the Apostles, may have exaggerated the intensity and extent of Jewish persecution of Christians. Part of the problem may lie in the English 'persecution' to denote what may often have been local friction, harassment and controversy.

became flesh'. So Jesus was in the world, very much part-and-parcel of it as a human being of flesh and blood. Christians need to read this Gospel discerningly, so that its strident language about the world does not lead them to adopt an attitude to the world which is semi-detached and stridently critical. Similarly, John's almost uniformly negative picture of 'the Jews' must not lead us to adopt a destructively critical view of the Jewish people either then or now.

Perhaps the most important response to be made to the potentially malign effects of John's language about 'the Jews' is to be sensitive to the problem. Whether the compilers of the lectionary now used in many British churches were right to 'censor' John 8, no Christian should read this dialogue between Jesus and 'the Jews' without a certain fear and trembling. Not least, Christians must continue to work and to pray for increasing understanding and goodwill between themselves and their Jewish brothers and sisters.

Conclusion

So are we sadly to conclude that John's Gospel is not as attractive as we thought? That this chapter has confirmed our worst suspicions of it? I hope neither is true. But the questions discussed here need to be faced. Christians would do well to stop describing themselves as 'in the world, but not of it'; such a description distorts our understanding of Christian existence, and fails to do justice to John's Gospel. It is more accurate, as I have argued, to turn the phrase round: 'not of this world, but sent into it' (as Jesus was).

Similarly, those inclined to be dismissive of feminist difficulties with the Bible need to pay sympathetic attention to them. At the same time, I hope it will be seen, both by feminist critics of the Bible and by those in the churches who perpetuate gender discrimination, that the New Testament, in its radical understanding of 'equality of regard', contains the seeds of a revolution yet to be fully realized in the Church and the wider world. John's Gospel, it must be said, gives to two women, Martha and Mary Magdalene, two extraordinarily important roles in the unfolding drama (11.27; 20.11–18), while its central metaphors of 'Father' and 'Son' for God and Jesus, while masculine in their literal sense, point – precisely because they are metaphors – beyond gender.

It is also time for Christians to stop using John 14.6 as a weapon against people of other faiths. To do so wrenches it from its context and distorts its emphasis. There are better ways of witnessing and evangelizing. As for John's negative portrayal of 'the Jews', it is vital that Christian readers recognize the problem, are sensitive to it, and allow John's rhetoric to work in them only good, and not ill.

What matters in all these four instances is where we position ourselves. If we retreat into church comfort zones, we shall not really see or hear what this Gospel is saying to us about the world *both* as the object of God's love *and* as a difficult, even threatening sphere of mission. If we regard people of other faiths as rivals, competitors, or threats, it will be tempting to use the Bible as ammunition, campaigning on the uniqueness of Jesus. There is a better way, and John's Gospel points us to it. Whether we find the Bible objectionable, or what others say about it objectionable, the group of writings in the New Testament which bear the name John still have one supremely important thing to say to us:

> Beloved, let us love one another, because love is from God; everyone who loves is born of God and knows God. Whoever does not love does not know God, for God is love. (1 John 4.7)

What matters is not so much what we make of the text, but what it makes of us.

4

A Transforming Revelation

This chapter brings us, in many ways, to the heart of our subject. We shall seek to build on the outlines and themes sketched in earlier chapters, filling in details drawn from successive sections of the Gospel. So it may be helpful, first, to summarize the journey we have travelled thus far.

Chapter 1 sought to offer three overviews of John's Gospel, taking its bearings from the Gospel's prologue; the story of a mission, a story of dramatic irony, and the story of a trial. In Chapter 2 we set off in search of the Beloved Disciple, the probable journey he had taken and some of the reasons why he had written a gospel rather different from Matthew, Mark and Luke. Chapter 3 was 'time out' from our main theme, but time out which was necessary if we are to avoid the charge of finding in this Gospel simply what we want to find. It is not easy to avoid falling into that trap whenever we read anything at all, whether it's the Bible or a newspaper, but it's important to try.

In Chapter 2 we asked the question whether John's Jesus is 'the real Jesus'. It is important not to duck that question, because most readers of the Gospels can hardly fail to notice the differences of detail in their portraits of Jesus between Matthew, Mark and Luke on the one hand, and John on the other. So the first section of this chapter will look at some of the characteristics of Jesus in John, drawing mainly on material taken from the earlier chapters of the Gospel.

The man from heaven

Fully human, fully divine?

There are widespread doubts today about whether Jesus was both human and divine in the way that the Church has traditionally claimed. People with little or no knowledge of the Christian faith may be inclined to associate Jesus with mythological characters or figures from science fiction. Even in the churches there are many who either reject or are deeply unsure about Jesus' divinity.

In the churches, too, people often struggle – not surprisingly – with how exactly Jesus could have been human and divine at the same time. I remember a student once proudly announcing that he had made some progress in sorting out his beliefs about Jesus; he had come to see that Jesus was 50 per cent human and 50 per cent divine. Two heresies in one go! It's worth recalling the classical formulation of this from the fifth century, the so-called 'Chalcedonian Definition' (though it is a statement about a mystery, rather than a definition that solves a problem). In this statement the Church declared that Jesus was *fully* human and *fully* divine: the humanity and divinity of Jesus co-existed in his one person 'without confusion, without change, without division, without separation'.[1]

In brief, that meant that neither the humanity or divinity of Jesus were diluted – still *fully* human, *fully* divine. At the same time, this did not produce a person who was a split personality: 'without division, without separation'. That was how the Church, some three and a half centuries after John, sought to express the mystery of the person of Jesus. Christians might reasonably assume that John's Gospel paved the way for later Christian orthodoxy; the New Testament writings, after all, were primary, authoritiative sources as the Church thrashed out what it believed about Jesus. But we must first listen to John on his own terms, without the later language of Christian creeds and doctrines obscuring the distinctiveness of what he has to say.

---

1 J. McIntyre, *The Shape of Christology*, 2nd edn, Edinburgh: T & T Clark, 1998, p. 94.

The go-between

Once past the prologue, what impression do we get of Jesus in the opening sections of John's Gospel? Jesus comes to John the Baptist, who testifies that he saw the Spirit (1.32–34). As we saw in Chapter 2, there is no explicit reference here to Jesus' baptism. The evangelist either leaves us to assume it or prefers not to mention it. 'On the next day' (1.35), John the Baptist sees Jesus, and his further testimony encourages two of his own disciples to follow Jesus.

The verses that follow are familiar, yet unfamiliar to those who know the other Gospels. Most of the names we recognize (Andrew, Peter, Philip), and the command 'Follow me' (v. 43) we have heard before. But here a revelation is taking place, a revelation the climax of which is yet to come in the encounter of Jesus with Nathaniel. This encounter takes readers to another level. In saying that Jesus had seen Nathaniel 'under the fig tree' (v. 48), before they had even met, the Gospel portrays Jesus as possessing a supernatural knowledge which exceeds anything we read about in the other Gospels – apart, perhaps, from the arrangements Jesus makes for his entry into Jerusalem and, later, for eating the Passover (Mark 11.1–6; 14.12–16). All four evangelists portray a Jesus who can read human hearts (for example John 2.24–25; Mark 2.6–8), but this is knowledge of a different order.

There follows the climax to the gradual revelation of Jesus to his disciples at the outset of his ministry: the promise of Jesus to Nathaniel: 'Very truly, I tell you, you will see heaven opened and the angels of God ascending and descending on the Son of Man' (v. 51).

So Jesus is presented at the outset as a mediator between heaven and earth. But, given that the prologue called Jesus God's *only* Son (1.18), we should probably correct 'a mediator' to '*the* mediator. He is the ladder revealed to Jacob in the first book of the Bible (Genesis 28.12). If we ask: was this ladder raised from earth to heaven, or lowered from heaven to earth, later verses make it very clear: the Son of Man first came down (3.13) as 'bread from heaven' (6.33). What is more he came down to give his life for the world (6.51).

But the image of a ladder implies two-way traffic. Does the Son of Man in this Gospel return to heaven? John occasionally talks of the Son of Man 'ascending' (for example 3.13; 6.62), but he uses other words too: the Son of Man will be 'lifted up' (3.14; 8.28) and 'glorified' (12.23). This will, indeed, ensure that a bridge between heaven and earth has been made: 'And I, when I am lifted up, will draw all people to myself' (12.32).

So there is good reason to call the Jesus of John's Gospel 'the man from heaven'. But do the feet of this heavenly visitor really touch the ground? That may seem an irreverent, unnecessary question to ask, but it needs to be asked because of the way the writer portrays Jesus.

A Jesus on his own terms

This Gospel of John is remarkably consistent in its portrayal of a Jesus who talks to people on his own terms, and does things in his own way and in his own time. The Jesus of this Gospel doesn't seem to converse with people in the way that other human beings do. When his mother asks for help at Cana, Jesus' reply seems to have nothing to do with the fact that the wine has run out: 'Woman, what concern is that to you and me? My hour has not yet come' (2.4). In chapter 3 he sweeps aside the 'flannel' of Nicodemus with a stern summons to be born again (3.2–3). In Samaria the disciples who left a weary (and hungry?) Jesus by the well at Sychar return with the shopping only to be told by their master that he has his own bread supply (3.5–8, 27, 31–34). A ruler asks him to come down to Capernaum to heal his son; Jesus responds, 'Unless you see signs and wonders you will not believe'; but the 'you' in Jesus' reply is plural, so who is Jesus talking to? No one else has been mentioned. (There are similar plurals in the conversation with Nicodemus: for example 'I say to you' (singular) but 'you [plural] do not receive our witness' (3.11.)

The most disconcerting example of Jesus doing things in his own time occurs in chapter 7. The brothers of Jesus urge him to go up to the Feast of Booths in Jerusalem, so that people there can see what he is doing. 'Show yourself to the world,' they said, and the evangelist comments, 'For not even his brothers believed in him' (vv. 4b, 5). It's clear that Jesus' family seem to have been ambivalent about his ministry (for example Mark 3.21), but it's hard to believe that they would have addressed Jesus in quite these terms. But what are we to make of Jesus' reply?

'Go to the festival yourselves. I am not going to this festival, for my time has not yet fully come.' After saying this, he remained in Galilee. But after his brothers had gone to the festival, then he also went, not publicly, but as it were in secret. (vv. 8–10)

Christian copyists of early manuscripts of this Gospel saw the problem; some altered verse 8 to read 'I am not *yet* going to this festival', and they or others added the phrase 'as it were' to verse 10 to lessen the contradiction with verse 8. We could argue that there was all the difference in the world between a public and a private, or secret, visit. A public visit might result in his death – but it wasn't time for his death ('my time has not yet fully come'). But even though Jesus went in secret according to verse 10, he was soon teaching in public (v. 14).

What are we to make of all this? There are no easy explanations. An early memory may lie behind this story. But it seems that the evangelist's wish to portray a Jesus who always works to his own agenda or, rather, his Father's agenda has resulted in a picture which, historically, does not seem very plausible.

There is another example. Martha and Mary send a message to Jesus informing him of their brother's serious illness. The story-line emphasizes Jesus' love for Lazarus and his sisters – and yet Jesus stayed where he was for two more days! It is another example of a Jesus who doesn't seem, in the language of Hebrews, 'like his brothers and sisters in every respect' (Hebrews 2.17).

Fully human?

If it's fair to say that there are times in this Gospel when Jesus' feet don't seem to touch the ground in the way that ordinary folks do, can we still say that the Jesus of John is truly human? Many of the human details found in the other Gospels are simply not here in John. In a passage that looks like this Gospel's equivalent of Jesus' prayer in Gethsemane in the other Gospels, Jesus acknowledges that his 'soul is troubled', and he wonders aloud whether he should pray 'Father save me from this hour' (12.27). But then it's almost as if John 'fast forwards' to the end of Jesus' anguish (as it is described in the other Gospels), because Jesus answers his own question: 'No, it is for this reason that I have come to this hour. Father, glorify your name' (vv. 27b, 28a). We might speculate that this was the outcome of Jesus' long vigil in Gethsemane. If so, John has chosen to concentrate on that, and to pass over the hours of anguished prayer which preceded it. (We noted in Chapter 2 that the prayer of Jesus in John 17 also lacks the anguish of the prayer in Gethsemane in Matthew, Mark and Luke.)

Yet interspersed throughout this picture of a Jesus who 'strides over the earth like a god'[2] are a few indications that this was a real human being. Heavenly visitor though he was, he experiences tiredness and thirst (4.6, 7), although even here the emphasis falls, not on the thirst of Jesus himself, but on everyone else's.

The most notable references to the humanness of Jesus occur in the story of the raising of Lazarus. When Jesus saw Mary and 'the Jews' weeping, 'he was greatly disturbed in spirit and deeply moved' (11.33). Moments later, we are told, 'Jesus began to weep' (v. 35), and 'Jesus, again, greatly disturbed came to the tomb' (v. 38). Whatever originally happened, these details anticipate the later suffering of Jesus, when he will lay down his life for his friends (15.13). The evangelist has already emphasized that Jesus loved Lazarus (vv. 3, 5, as well as v. 36); now, he indicates that only through the suffering of Jesus will Lazarus receive new life.

The distinctiveness of John

In trying to understand John's portrait of this 'man from heaven', we may find it helpful to recall how his Gospel probably evolved

2 The phrase comes from E. Käsemann's thought-provoking book *The Testament of Jesus*, London: SCM, 1968.

over several decades. We can reasonably assume that it originated at a time when many people remembered Jesus. His humanity was simply taken for granted. As time went by, Christian experience, and particularly their faith in the resurrection of Jesus, will have cast his life in new light. But in John's case, his particular agenda – of focusing on the God-given credentials and ultimate identity of Jesus – led him to pass over some of the human details we find in Matthew, Mark and Luke. Only in the final stages of the Gospel's evolution, in a Greek environment, was it thought necessary to emphasize what hardly anyone now living could recall, that Jesus had been a real human being: the Word really was 'made flesh'.

So, despite differences of emphasis here and there – now on his 'flesh-and-blood' humanity, but more often on his divine origins and destiny – the man from heaven fulfils his mission and returns to where he has come from, namely, the Father. This is the third stage: the Son of Man came down from heaven (first stage), spoke the words his Father had given him (12.49–50, second stage), and now the Son returns to the Father (third stage). And so the 'ladder' to which Jesus refers near the beginning of this Gospel (1.51) is firmly in place. Only then can Simon Peter and others follow Jesus (13. 36). He has gone to prepare a place for them (14.1). Although those words are read at funeral services, and rightly so, we need to recognize a broader and deeper meaning in them. In the words of Irenaeus, the second-century Church father: 'Because of his measureless love, he became what we are, in order to enable us to become what He is.'[3]

A post-Easter perspective

If we are not to be misled by John's Gospel, we need to recognize how thoroughly the author's belief in the resurrection and divinity of Jesus pervades his presentation of Jesus' life and teaching. We sometimes talk – mistakenly – of achieving a 'balance'

---

3 Irenaeus, *Adv. Haer.* V, quoted in Frances Young, *The Making of the Creeds*, London: SCM, 1991, new edn 2002, p. 84.

between the humanity and divinity of Jesus. If that is the test, John fails miserably. This is not the best way to approach the mystery of Jesus Christ, as if the more human Jesus was, the less divine he must have been, and vice versa. Orthodoxy's insistence that Jesus was wholly human and wholly divine is not a balance!

This is the most important example of John carrying on where the other Gospels leave off. The growing Christian belief that Jesus was somehow God 'all through' thoroughly permeates John's portrait of Jesus. For all the very human, down-to-earth details still there, we are looking more at a figure in a stained-glass window, or a Christ in one of the great renaissance paintings. But perhaps this is why God in his good providence steered the Church to include four Gospels, not just one, in its Scriptures.

The gift of life

'The man from heaven' does not come empty handed. He comes with a gift, described in various ways in the Gospel: it is bread (6.35, 48), light (8.12; 9.5), freedom (8.32, 36). Most frequently, however, the gift is described as life, or eternal life, defined quite simply as the knowledge of God and of 'Jesus Christ whom you sent' (17.5). So 'the man from heaven' may properly be called a transforming presence. The wedding scene at Cana expresses, in one parable-like event, Jesus' entire life's work. Its conclusion (2.11) shows what divine revelation truly means: the transformation of human life. But, as the Gospel goes on to narrate, not everyone, by any means, welcomes with open arms this gift of light and life.

A growing rift?

If we were asked to say which chapters of John's Gospel we knew least well, or found most difficult, I imagine chapters 5 to 8 would be high on the list of most of us. There are several reasons for this: the chapters are long, their subject matter is not easy to grasp, and the controversies in which Jesus is engaged get increasingly acrimonious.

It's important to remember the argument of Chapter 3, when we looked at the apparent anti-Jewishness of the Gospel, and particularly its very negative portrayal of 'the Jews'. This section of John's Gospel, more than any others, reflects the arguments and conflicts about Jesus between Church and synagogue. John's Gospel evolved over time in a way that makes it difficult, if not impossible, to separate out what Jesus originally said and did from the later reflections and additions of the evangelist. So we should bracket out of our minds questions such as 'What exactly happened?' or 'Did Jesus really say that?' As we have seen in the course of this book, history merges almost seamlessly with later Christian reflection, and we don't necessarily need to disentangle the two.

A healing and its sequel (John 5)

In the immediate sequel to the healing of the lame man by the pool of Bethzatha, 'the Jews' accuse Jesus of making himself equal with God (v. 18), and Jesus responds with the first extended teaching in this Gospel about 'the Father' and 'the Son' (vv. 19–23). Here we could almost be in the carpenter's shop in Nazareth:[4] 'the Son can do nothing on his own, but only what he sees the Father doing' (v. 19). A son depends on his father, learns from and copies his father. What are the 'greater things' (v. 20) which the Father will show the Son? Raising the dead and giving them life and judgement. These are the prerogatives of God. But here we are told that 'the Son' will share in them (vv. 21–22). (The biblical theme of judging is one that we tend to ignore or to misunderstand, and I shall return to this later.)

So Jesus is given authority to do two things. The first is to 'give life to whomsoever he wishes' (v. 21). That sounds unpleasantly arbitrary, as if a person's salvation depends on a divine whim. But other verses (for example 17.21, 23) in this Gospel show that God intends to be neither arbitrary nor selective. The second

---

4 C. H. Dodd first drew attention to the possibility that the language of John 5.19–20 might reflect the experience of Jesus in a carpenter's workshop in Nazareth.

thing the Son will do is to judge. This is a searching thought and we should not try to avoid it, or to play it down. It is a judgement that is taking place now, and which will also happen in the future (vv. 25, 28). In fact, the last judgement has already begun to happen with the coming of the light into the world. What will be the basis of that judgement? There are two criteria here: have people heard 'the voice of the Son of God' (v. 25), and have they done good or evil (v. 29)?

These two activities – giving life and passing judgement – are the prerogatives of the Creator. How is it that Jesus can assume them? But he does not 'assume' them; the Son does nothing without the Father; if he did, it wouldn't be true or valid. The Father stands behind the Son *in everything* (v. 37). (See the earlier discussion in Chapter 1 of the authority behind the mission.) God has entrusted everything to the Son, so that humankind is called to honour him, and called to honour the Father (v. 23).

So we have met what will be a recurring theme in John: the Son's humble dependence on the Father, and his obedience to his divinely given mandate: 'I can do nothing on my own' and 'I seek to do not my own will but the will of him who sent me' (v. 30). Here, in one simple phrase, are Jesus' entire credentials: the Father sent him. But already there are signs that the mission of Jesus is encountering opposition. Jesus offers a bleak assessment of where 'the Jews' stand with God: 'And the Father who sent me has himself testified on my behalf. You have never heard his voice or seen his form, and you do not have his word abiding in you, because you do not believe him whom he has sent' (5.37–38).

I argued in the last chapter that verses such as these which are so critical of 'the Jews' should not be read as if they were a straightforward account of what actually happened, even though we know from the other Gospels that Jesus' ministry encountered fierce opposition from Jewish leaders, if not others. In any case, Jesus is not dismissing, distorting or riding roughshod over the spiritual heritage of the Jewish people. On the contrary, that heritage points to him: their own Scriptures testify to him (vv. 39, 45–47). So they stand condemned by their own tradition, as, indeed, many 'Christians' are condemned by Christian tradition today. We miss the challenge of John's harsh words about 'the Jews', unless we see that they point to the deepest issue of all: whether a world turned in on itself, and preoccupied with externals rather than with the invisible God will find its deepest well-being and life (vv. 34, 40) by turning to the One who now speaks through his Son.

So here are words of challenge and judgement: the coming of the light obliges people to choose. Dramatic as it may sound, it is a choice between the way of life and the way of death. (As I pointed out in Chapter 1, this Gospel says nothing about hell and eternal punishment.)

Bread and the Bread of Life (John 6)

Chapter 6 opens in Galilee,[5] with two stories which, at first sight, seem familiar: the feeding of the five thousand (6.1–15) and Jesus walking on the water (6.16–21). But John has put his own stamp on both stories. In the feeding miracle, Jesus takes the initiative from start to finish. He, not the disciples, asks where they are to buy bread to feed the crowd (v. 5); remarkably, he, not the disciples, distributes the bread and fish to the assembled company (v.11) and, finally, he instructs the disciples to gather up the food left over (v. 12).

In John's version of Jesus walking on the water, the miracle does not include, as in Mark and Matthew, the miraculous abating of the wind, even though John's reference to the wind (v. 18) might lead us to expect that. Instead, the miracle in John is the appearance of Jesus walking on the water, and their instant arrival at their destination as soon as he had revealed himself to them (vv. 20–21). But Jesus' words here, though almost exactly the same as in Mark (Mark 6.50), already have a deeper resonance: 'It is me; do not be afraid.'[6]

---

5 The geography of John 5–7 seems a little odd, prompting some scholars to wonder whether chapter 6 was inserted at a relatively late stage in the development of the Gospel.

6 See Chapter 5 below.

The crowd, naturally puzzled on their return to Capernaum to find Jesus had got there before them, ask him, 'Rabbi, when did you come here?' (6.22–25). Their question provides the opening for a long section of teaching about the bread of life. Jesus' immediate response, 'You are looking for me, not because you saw signs, but because you ate your fill of the loaves' (v. 26), seems strange at first. Surely the crowd *did* see a miracle, and that is why they are looking for him? But a sign points beyond itself to what it signifies; that is what all the 'signs' in this Gospel do, and some people see where they are pointing – that is to Jesus – and some do not (for example 11.45–46). So here, if the crowd have merely had a good meal, and not perceived the Bread of Life in their midst, they have missed the life-giving revelation at the heart of the meal.

More questions from 'the Jews' follow. What do they have to do (v. 28)? What proof will Jesus provide so that they can believe in him (v. 30)? If this bread really does come from heaven, could they have it (vv. 33–34)? More sceptically, if this man is the son of Joseph, how can he possibly say, 'I have come down from heaven' (v. 42)? In reply, Jesus – as John portrays him – is unwearyingly focused and repetitive: God, not Moses, supplied the bread from heaven, which now *is* the One who descends from heaven (v. 33), and the one thing necessary is to believe in him (v. 29).

Belief is not something a person can manufacture at will. Only God can 'draw' people to his Son, and teach them (vv. 44–45). But even here, with such an emphasis on God's initiative in creating belief in human lives, a wider perspective remains: the One who has descended from heaven gives life, not just to a chosen few, but to the world (vv. 33, 51). Life, both here and hereafter, is what is at stake: the one who eats this bread does not die (v. 50), *and* Jesus will raise them up 'on the last day' (vv. 39–40).

So Jesus is the bread that comes from heaven, removes hunger (v. 35), and gives eternal life (vv. 33, 35, 48, 51). And all this Jesus does as the Son, acting in obedience to his Father (v. 40) and as the Son of Man (v. 27) who brings heaven to earth and unites earth to heaven.

The argument is both dense and repetitive, and it is not surprising that modern readers of the Gospel find chapters like this difficult to read and follow. It is difficult partly because the many repetitions do more than merely repeat what has already been said; they go on to say more. This is particularly so in a final section (vv. 52–58), where the allusions to the Christian sacrament of Holy Communion are unmistakable.

Even some of his disciples find this teaching too hard. The evangelist seems to mean the explicit language about eating flesh and drinking blood (vv. 53–56). But behind that offensive language is the even more offensive reality of the cross. That is the force of Jesus' response to these disciples: 'Does this offend you? Then what if you were to see the Son of Man ascending to where he was before?' (vv. 61b, 62).

Judas and the problem of evil

The final verses of this chapter, particularly the dark references to Judas, highlight again the mystery of why some people believe and some do not. It cannot be entirely explained on the human level, as if it is just a matter of making the correct choice. So Simon Peter's acknowledgement of Jesus as the life-giving Holy One of God (vv. 68–69) is not to his credit, but a gift from God. Conversely, there is a divine providence at work even in Judas' betrayal of Jesus, because even the devil, it is implied, serves the purposes of God (vv. 70–71). This sounds unfair to Judas, giving the impression that he was no more than a puppet of both God and the devil. But this may have been what a distinguished theologian meant when he said that Judas '*was* the problem of evil'. He didn't mean that the disciple was evil incarnate, but that in his betrayal are focused the difficult questions of human free will and responsibility, and the place of evil in the purpose and providence of God.

We need to avoid simplistic answers to questions like these. God in his love does not deprive human beings of their free will and autonomy. Yet nothing happens outside his gracious sovereignty either; God is the infinitely resourceful opportunist. The New Testament gives two answers to the question: Who handed

Jesus over to suffering and to death? Its answers are 'God' (for example Romans 8.32) and 'Judas'. As for Judas' tragic end, I find it helpful to recall St Augustine's reflection on the tradition that Judas committed suicide (Matthew 27.3–10; Acts 1.18–19): the real failure of Judas was to despair of the mercy of God. Even more thought-provoking is the child's response to the question: Where was Jesus between Good Friday and Easter Day? 'Looking for his friend Judas.'

Controversies in Jerusalem: John 7

The scene changes once more, as Jesus returns to Jerusalem, this time for the Feast of Tabernacles (7.14), following the conversation between Jesus and his brothers (discussed in the last section). Some themes from chapter 5 are replayed and developed. But now the debate begins to focus on Jesus from a new angle: is he, or is he not, the Christ (the Messiah)? Earlier in his Gospel, the evangelist was at pains to emphasize that John the Baptist was not the Messiah (1.20, 25; 3.28), and Jesus was (1.41; 4.25–26). The debates in Jerusalem which now follow (7.25–27) have an authentic ring about them, though John as usual has stamped his own style unmistakably on them. One of the hallmarks of his style, as we saw (Chapter 1), was a certain dramatic irony, as here in the words of the Jerusalem public: 'Yet we know where this man is from; but when the Messiah comes, no one will know where he is from' (v. 27).

As often in John, much of chapter 7 seems to be a suggestive interweaving of the evangelist's own reflections with older themes from the other Gospels. How does he know the law so well without a formal education? 'the Jews' want to know (v. 15). The answer is that Jesus' wisdom is God-given, as people whose lives are oriented towards God will recognize (vv. 16–17). Jesus' transparency to God involves a complete negation of self and self-seeking; this is why he is utterly real (v. 18) – and, we might add, so disturbing a presence in the world.

Another charge against Jesus, familiar from the other Gospels, now follows: 'You have a demon!' (v. 20). Jesus' reply, with its reference to 'one work', performed on the Sabbath (vv. 21–23), takes us back to chapter 5 (almost as though the intervening chapter were not there): Jesus' opponents circumcise a man on the Sabbath, so why shouldn't Jesus heal on that day? The real issue, Jesus goes on to say, is seeing properly, and therefore coming to a right judgement: 'Do not judge by appearances, but judge with right judgement' (v. 24).

The arguments about Jesus in Jerusalem continue; the authorities want to kill him, and yet Jesus continues to teach. Is this because the powers that be realize he is the Messiah (vv. 25–26)? But John, as usual, develops the discussions in a way that takes his readers to the heart of the matter: *where is Jesus from?* They think they know (v. 27), but Jesus, calling out, like Wisdom in the street (Proverbs 8.1–4), insists that God, whom they do not know, has sent him (v. 29). So blunt a summary of the fundamental issue divides the crowd; some believe in Jesus, some seek to arrest him but, the writer tells us, the time for that has not yet come (vv. 30–31).

The Pharisees, in alliance with the chief priests, try to arrest Jesus (v. 32). Jesus responds in language which will recur in his final words to his disciples: 'I will be with you a little while longer, and then I am going to him who sent me. You will search for me, but you will not find me; and where I am you cannot come' (vv. 33–34, compare 13.33; 16.5–7; 8.21). After more misunderstanding (v. 35), Jesus issues his invitation to life once more: 'If anyone is thirsty, let him come to me, and let the one who believes in me drink' (vv. 37b, 38a).

Still more discussion about Jesus ensues: how can he be the Messiah, if he comes from Galilee (v. 41)? After all, the Messiah is supposed to come from Bethlehem (v. 42). Is this ironic as well? John doesn't mention, even if he knows, the tradition that Jesus was born in Bethlehem. And still no one lays a hand on Jesus, even though they would dearly love to do so (v. 43).

Nicodemus, one of their own number (v. 50), is involved in the final argument here. 'You're not from Galilee as well, are you?' they ask him. Tellingly, the discussion ends with a double entendre: (literally) 'a prophet from Galilee is not raised' (v. 52). '*Is not raised*'? How little do they know!

Beauty and ugliness (John 8)

The story of the woman taken in adultery (8.1–11) is a late addition – perhaps in the second century – to John's Gospel. But, even if John did not write it, its beauty and power and, not least, its similarity to other stories about Jesus in the other Gospels, make a compelling case for its inclusion in John.

Late inclusion though it is, the story graphically illustrates what this Gospel repeatedly says: God did not send his Son into the world to condemn it, but to save it (3.17; 8.15; 12.47). This takes some grasping. It goes against many of our perceptions and gut-feelings about God: God does not approve of us, and we're not really surprised. Or, if we are religious but only superficially touched by the gospel, we expect God to disapprove of all the people of whom we disapprove. So this is a story of the God of surprises.

After this story, John seems to resume where he had left off – with Jesus at the Feast of Tabernacles. And, because lights were a prominent feature of that feast, we should not be surprised to hear Jesus saying, 'I am the light of the world' (8.12), a claim repeated in the next chapter (9.5). The dialogues that follow, first, between Jesus and the Pharisees (from v. 13) and then between Jesus and 'the Jews' (from v. 22), focus once more on the most crucial issue of all: Jesus' relationship with 'the Father', the One who sent him (vv. 16, 18); in other words, where has Jesus come from and where is he going (v. 14)?

Does this entitle Jesus to talk about himself? Yes and no. No, if he speaks 'off his own bat', without the authority of the Father. That is what Jesus had said before (5.31), words which the Pharisees now quote back at him. Yet Jesus may speak about himself, if his mandate from God is real, and any judgement he passes is valid for the same reason (v. 16); Father and Son unite in a common witness (v. 17), and the question of his opponents, 'Where is your father?' merely demonstrates their ignorance (v. 19).

The conversation switches to the spiritual and moral status of Jesus' opponents. The gulf between them and him could hardly be wider; it's the gulf between 'below' and 'above', between the world and God (v. 23). The question is inevitable: 'Who are you?' (v. 25). But that question can only be answered with reference to the Father, from whom Jesus takes his entire bearings, and who confers on Jesus his unique status (vv. 26, 28, 29).

Things now move to a tragic climax. Although many Jews believed in Jesus (vv. 30–31), the discussion which follows shows that their faith is superficial. They have taken the first step towards life and freedom, but they fall back on their status as children of Abraham (v. 33, 39). Contrary to what they suppose, says Jesus, their real father is the devil (v. 44). This is the severest judgement of all, and a statement which we might wish John had never written. (See the earlier discussion in Chapter 3.) Yet even this – because the devil is 'the father of lies' – points up the profound difference between truth and lies, reality and unreality: the opponents of Jesus are trapped in their own unreal world, and cannot hear what Jesus is saying to them (vv. 43, 47).

Conclusion

It would not be surprising if chapters 5 – 8 of the Gospel are the least well known. The discourses in these chapters not only sound acrimonious; they are long and confusing, because they repeat and develop themes at the same time. Whether a 'growing rift' accurately describes these chapters is an interesting question. It may be more correct to say that God's revelation is met from the outset by incomprehension and hostility. And that is the world's responsibility. As for God's response, even though Jesus is portrayed here as pulling no punches, later chapters will show that all is not lost.

Community of love

The public ministry of Jesus has still some way to go; 12.44–50 provides a final summing up. But there is no mistaking a new development from the beginning of chapter 9. The opposition to Jesus rumbles on – indeed, builds up – but now disciples and friends of Jesus begin to appear. We start to glimpse the

beginnings of a new community. The healing of the blind man
(9.1–41) is also the story of how this man became a disciple of
Jesus. Lazarus (John 11) is not only a man brought back to life,
but someone whose function in this Gospel is that of a representative disciple. For Lazarus readers may substitute themselves,
or the Church.

Shepherd and sheep: John 10

Not surprisingly, sandwiched between these stories of people
given new life by Jesus, there is a discourse about a new community. Admittedly, controversy returns, even in John 10 (from v.
19), but not before a 'parable' about the Good Shepherd and his
sheep. Jewish 'readers' of the Gospel could hardly fail to compare and contrast these words of Jesus with the moving portrait
of God in Ezekiel 34. After a searing condemnation of 'the shepherds of Israel' who have neglected the sheep (compare 'the hired
shepherds' of John 10.12), the passage in Ezekiel goes on:

> For thus says the Lord God: I myself will search for my sheep,
> and will seek them out . . . I myself will be the shepherd of my
> sheep, and I will make them lie down, says the Lord God. I
> will seek the lost, and I will bring back the strayed, and I will
> bind up the injured, and I will strengthen the weak, but the
> fat and the strong I will destroy. I will feed them with justice.
> (Ezekiel 34.11, 15–16)

So Jesus is, or will be to 'the sheep', all that God was and is. But
the Gospel goes further than the prophet in its repeated insistence that this good shepherd 'lays down his life' for the sheep
(John 10.11, 15). Later, as Jesus washes his disciples' feet, John
describes his actions in words probably intended to recall this
passage: he 'lays down' his clothes and 'takes them up' again
(13.4, 12).

Before we leave the parable, there are two other points to note.
First, Jesus has a dual role: he is the 'gate' for the sheep (vv.1–3, 7)
and he is also the shepherd. How is this possible? The answer

probably lies in this Gospel's dual emphasis *both* on the Son's obedience to and dependence on the Father, *and* his equality and unity with the Father ('the Father and I are one', v. 30). We also hear of 'other sheep' (v. 16). Who are these? The evangelist later explains: they will be those 'gathered into one', presumably Gentiles together with the people of Israel (11.52).

'The hour': John 11 – 12

So 'the hour' inexorably approaches. Jesus enters the heart of his own realm (Jerusalem, 12.12–16), dividing 'the Jews' into those who believed in him and those who wanted to murder him (11.53; 12.9–11). At the same time, the contours are emerging of a new community whose parameters will be worldwide. That may be the symbolism behind the detail of 12.3: the aroma of the ointment which Mary uses to anoint Jesus fills the house. The point becomes clearer still in the grumble of the Pharisees, which anticipates or reflects what was happening by the time this Gospel was written: 'Look, the world has gone after him!' (12.19).

Their words are the cue for the entry of 'some Greeks' who want to see Jesus (12.20). Two disciples, Andrew and Philip, report their request to Jesus who, as so often in this Gospel, seems to see beyond the immediate request (compare 2.3–4 and 4.47–48). Is he saying 'Yes' or 'No' to the Greeks' request in his response: 'The hour has come for the Son of Man to be glorified' (v. 23)? What Jesus goes on to say supplies the answer: 'Very truly, I tell you, unless a grain of wheat falls into the earth and dies, it remains just a single grain; but if it dies it bears much fruit' (v. 24). A saying at the end of this story confirms just how fruitful his death will be: 'I, when I am lifted up from the earth, will draw all people to myself' (v. 32 explained by v. 33).

So the Son's mission approaches its climax, and the world, unbeknown to itself, faces its moment of truth: 'Now is the judgement of this world; now the ruler of this world will be driven out' (12.31).

In the five chapters that follow (John 13 – 18), we can just see the storyline of the other Gospels: Jesus eats with his disciples (but

not the Passover meal – contrast, for example, Mark 14.12–25),
Judas betrays Jesus (13.18–30), Peter will deny him (13.38), and
the disciples will be scattered, leaving Jesus alone (13.38). But,
almost submerging this storyline, is Jesus' farewell discourse to
his disciples, and his prayer to his Father (14.1—17.2).

The dual perspective of the farewell discourses: John 14—16

As usual in this Gospel, these chapters, we may assume, are
a thorough 'mix' of Jesus' original words and the evangelist's
development of them. There are clear echoes here of Jesus' teaching in the other Gospels, particularly in the repeated (and variously worded) promise that whatever they ask they will receive
(14.13–14; 15.7, 16; 16.23, compare, for example, Luke 11.9,
though John's versions usually carry the additional phrase 'in my
name'). Yet there can be little doubt that original words of Jesus
have been woven into a much larger tapestry by the inspired
imagination of the evangelist (drawing, no doubt, on the teaching of 'the beloved disciple').

One or two other preliminary remarks will help us capture the
perspective of these chapters. The Bible has many farewell discourses, as we briefly noted in Chapter 1. All of them, whether
Jacob's (Genesis 49.1–27) or Moses' (Deuteronomy 1—30;
31.1–2, etc.) or Paul's (Acts 20.17–35), were intended to prepare
the families or followers of these leaders for what was to come.
It was a well-known genre of the ancient world: the last will and
testament, as it were, of a great figure of the past.

The purpose of a farewell discourse of preparing the teacher's
disciples for what is to come is very clear in John's Gospel: 'And
now I have told you this before it occurs, so that when it does
occur, you may believe' (14.29, compare 16.1–4, 31–33).

So farewell discourses like these have two settings: the lifetime
of the leader whose farewell speech it is, and also the life-setting,
with all its challenges and problems, of the followers for whom
the speech is given. It is not difficult to see the dual perspective of
John's last discourses. One setting – Jesus' own lifetime – is clearly

reflected in a verse such as 14.25: 'I have said these things to you while I am still with you' (14.25). But other verses reflect, or hint at, a later time: 'I did not say these things to you from the beginning, because I was with you' (16.4b). There is the same dual perspective in the prayer of Jesus: 'And now I am no longer in the world . . .' (17.11) and ' . . . while I was with them' (17.12).

Father, Son and Spirit: parallels

But now we turn to the main themes, which are replayed over and over, so that disciples need be left in no doubt about the fundamental challenges they face, but also so that they know beyond doubt what is promised to them so that they can meet those challenges. We begin where the discourses themselves begin – with the extraordinary parallelism in the language used of the Father and the Son. So the disciples are invited to believe in Jesus as they believe in God (14.1). Conversely, they are assured that, because they have come to know Jesus, they now know the Father, that if they have seen Jesus, they have seen the Father too (14.7, 9).

There are still more parallels between God and Jesus, as there have been throughout this Gospel: for example, 'whoever hates me, hates my Father also' (15.23). Does the Gospel give us a deeper glimpse of this unity between Father and Son? Yes, it does. Jesus invites his disciples to believe that 'I am in the Father and the Father is in me' (14.11, compare 10.38). But what kind of language is this? It has been described as the language of love, and that is an important part of the truth. But not even two human beings deeply in love with each other are likely to use this language of mutual indwelling. It is a *spiritual* expression and, as such, it is language about an experience of God. The writings that bear John's name give us two sublimely simple yet profound statements about God: God is Spirit (4.24) and God is love (1 John 4.8, 16). These verses are the key to the language here about being 'in the Father' and 'the Father in me'.

But now we must notice another remarkable series of parallels – this time between Jesus and One variously described as an

'Advocate' (14.16, 26; 15.26; 16.7), 'the Spirit of truth' (14.17; 15.26; 16.13) and 'the Holy Spirit' (14.26). The Holy Spirit in this Gospel has been well described as Jesus' 'double'; the Spirit carries on where Jesus, so to speak, left off. So for example, the Spirit 'testifies' on Jesus' behalf (15.26) as Jesus testified to God (3.32), and the Spirit will 'convict the world of sin' (16.7–8) as Jesus did (for example 8.21–24).

Promises and challenges

So when we turn to the many promises in Jesus' farewell discourse, it is natural to begin with one which refers to Spirit, Son and Father. Jesus promises the disciple that the Spirit will come and be 'in them' (14.16–17, 26–27; 15.26). He also promises that he himself will come to them (for example 14.3). But even this is not all. To those who love him he promises 'my Father will love them, and we will come to them and make our home with them' (14.23).What will the coming of the Spirit, Son and Father to the disciple actually mean? Here we must note the way in which the language of love and of God ('I in the Father and the Father in me') is, in this Gospel, *extended*: 'On that day you will know that I am in my Father, and you in me, and I in you' (14.20). There are many more verses that repeat and develop this extraordinary language, particularly the passage which begins with the claim 'I am the true vine': 'abide in me as I abide in you' (15.4). That command seems to mean 'Abide in my love' (15.9). Jesus in this Gospel has already spoken in this way (6.56), and he will do so again in his prayer: 'I ask . . . that they may all be one. As you, Father, are in me and I am in you, may they also be in us' (17.20–1; compare v. 23).

We are looking here at remarkable language which is a kind of God-language, and so language which is also the language of love and spirit – the language of communion. It sounds as though God is extending himself to include us. Or, as someone once expressed it, the death of Jesus is the moment when God the Father and God the Son moved sufficiently far apart to accommodate the whole world in between.

So this is the first promise, the key to all the others: Father, Son and Holy Spirit make their home in us; we are 'included' in them. From this starting-point, the promises almost tumble over one another. There will be a place for them in the Father's house (14.2–3) both now and hereafter. From now on, they will know and see the Father (14.7, 9). They will do 'greater works than these' (14.12), a promise which is puzzling in its apparent claim that the disciples will outdo Jesus. The disciples will receive the peace of Jesus (14.27), the joy of Jesus (15.11); because he lives, they will live (14.19); because he 'conquered the world' (16.33), it is clearly implied that they will too.

This is not an exhaustive list of the promises made to the disciples here. But now we must turn to the commands. Although Jesus twice refers to his 'commands' – that is plural – those commands, it seems, reduce to two: the commands to obey and to love (for example 14.21; 15.17). But there is another command overarching the entire discourse, and repeated within it: 'Do not let your hearts be troubled' (14.1, 27) and, finally, 'In the world you face persecution. But take courage; I have conquered the world!' (16.33).

There is one more perspective to notice. A disciple is portrayed as enquiring how it is that Jesus will reveal himself to them and not to the world (14.22), and Jesus refers him to the 'coming' of God, Father and Son, to indwell the disciple (v. 23). A later verse returns to the theme of revelation and of the seeing which accompanies revelation: 'A little while, and you will no longer see me, and again a little while and you will see me' (16.16).

What is this 'little while'? The disciples themselves ask this question (16.17–19). Once more, we need to recall the dual perspectives of this Gospel. This 'little while' is undoubtedly, in the first place, the interval of time between the crucifixion and the resurrection; in this interval 'you will weep and mourn, but the world will rejoice' (v. 20). But 'the little while' is also, I think, the interval between the time of Jesus and his final 'coming', whenever and however that will be. Unlike the other Gospels, John's Gospel has no clear references to what Christian tradition has called the 'second coming' (though see 21.23).

But perhaps it is implied here: 'and again a little while and you will see me'.

A prayer on the threshold of heaven: John 17

What Jesus promises his disciples in chapters 14—16 provides the key to what he prays for and about them in chapter 17. They will be gathered up into his life and mission. Most extraordinary of all, they will receive the glory which God gave to Jesus (17.22), not for their own gratification or glory, but so that the world may know and come to believe. They have come to know the very name of God (v. 26) and, in case we should think that this is some esoteric, unworldly secret, these chapters end with the language of love and of communion which has permeated them: 'that the love with which you have loved me may be in them, and I in them' (17.26).

Conclusion

Although the opposition to Jesus continues through chapters 9—12, a new process has emerged: God is creating a new community, illuminated by the light of revelation (chapter 9), its members called by name (chapter 10) and raised to new life (chapter 11). The new community will be universal in its scope (chapter 12), because the impending death of Jesus will bear much fruit (12.24). In succeeding chapters (chapters 13—17) we seem to enter an inner sanctum from which 'the world' is excluded, and where we are privileged to eavesdrop not only farewell commands and promises, but a prayer which spans earth and heaven.

'And we saw his glory': the Gospel's climax

Should we call chapters 18—20 the climax of this Gospel? In many ways they are: the Son fulfils his mission and the Gospel's dramatic irony reaches a climax as 'the world', oblivious of its own guilt, condemns and executes Jesus, incarnate Word of the world's Creator. Most of all, however, the Gospel's prologue is completed, as only now can it be said 'We have seen his glory.'

We noted earlier (Chapter 1) how the preceding chapters, John 13 — 17, outline in advance the meaning of the trial, crucifixion and resurrection narrated in chapters 18 — 20. We now examine these chapters in more detail, with an eye, as far as we can, to what the evangelist himself wants us to see.

The arrest of Jesus

The similarity of John to the other Gospels in his account of Jesus' arrest, trial and crucifixion is greater than at most other points in his story – with occasional exceptions, such as the feeding of the five thousand (6.1–15). But there are often details not found in Matthew, Mark or Luke. For example, only John mentions the brook Cedron (18.1), and it's only John who, in narrating the episode of a disciple stabbing a servant of the high priest, names the disciple as Peter and the injured man as Malchus (18.10–11). At the same time, we see the writer's distinctive touches everywhere.

John's distinctiveness is particularly apparent in his account of Jesus' arrest (18.1–11). As always in John, Jesus takes the initiative. Instead of Judas signalling by his kiss who is to be arrested, Jesus 'comes forward', asks who they are looking for, and to the expected answer 'Jesus of Nazareth' responds 'I am he' (vv. 4–5). Those words in the original Greek, however, constitute one of John's most powerful double entendres: *ego eimi* has come to mean, in the course of this Gospel, far more than just 'It's me'. They reflect the authority and even the divinity of Jesus (see Chapter 5), as the response of the arresting party indicates: 'When Jesus said to them "I am he", they stepped back and fell to the ground' (v. 6).

The trial of Jesus?

To those who knew one of the other Gospels, what follows would be a mixture of the familiar and the unfamiliar. So Jesus' appearance before the high priest they knew; only Matthew

(26.57) names him as Caiaphas, but only John mentions that Jesus appeared before both Annas and Caiaphas (18.13, 24).[7] Similarly, Peter's denial of Jesus is narrated by the other evangelists, but only John refers to 'another disciple' who enabled Peter to gain entrance to the high priest's courtyard (18.15–16), and only John splits the story of Peter into two parts (18.17–18, 25–27), contrasting his frightened denials with the bold testimony of Jesus (18.19–24).

John's version of Jesus before the high priest – in this case, Annas – is shorter than Mark's and Matthew's (John 18.19–24; Mark 14.55–64; Matthew 26.59–66) and, unlike them, doesn't focus on Jesus' Messiahship at all. Instead, this evangelist seems to want to give much greater prominence to Jesus' appearance before Pilate (18.28–19.16). This dramatic scene must be largely, if not entirely, an imaginative reconstruction, but no less powerful and inspired than a more historical account.

Pilate, powerful representative of the Roman Empire, declares Jesus innocent, and indicates his wish to release him (19.4, 12). Yet Pilate is under the illusion that he has more power than he really possesses: 'Do you not know that I have power to release you, and power to crucify you?' (v. 10). Jesus' reply puts Pilate in his place (v. 11). In fact, the reader can hardly miss the irony which runs throughout: who is really on trial here? The nub of the matter, as always, is the identity of Jesus and where he comes from – expressed here in the language of 'king' and 'kingdom'.

The first exchange between Jesus and Pilate (18.33–38) results in Jesus' declaration of what this Gospel has repeatedly emphasized: 'For this I was born and for this I came into the world, to testify to the truth' (v. 37).

At this stage, Pilate is contemptuous; 'What is truth?' (v. 38). But when he hears, via 'the Jews', Jesus' claim to be the Son of

---

7 John's account is a little puzzling at this point, with a brief reference to Jesus being taken to Annas 'first' (18.13), followed by an explanation that he was the father-in-law of Caiaphas, who was the high priest 'that year' (vv. 13b–14). But subsequent verses also refer to Annas as high priest (see 18.19, 24).

God, 'he was more afraid than ever' (19.7–8), and now poses the question which, for this evangelist, is the supremely important one: 'Where are you from?' (19.9).

Yet this is not so much the trial of Jesus, as his coronation. The writer's deft touches hint as much. First, Pilate presents Jesus to the crowd wearing purple and a crown of thorns, with the announcement, 'Here is the man!' (19.5). Again, John's choice of words (*anthropos* – human being – rather than *aner* – man) suggests that there is a deeper significance here. After further questioning, Pilate brings Jesus outside once more. Once again, the evangelist's language is teasingly ambiguous: does Pilate sit, or does he seat Jesus (19.13)? The NRSV notes that the Greek could mean either: perhaps the writer intended it to be so.

And so, with the terseness and brevity typical of the other Gospel writers, John, too, informs us that Jesus was handed over to be crucified (19.16).

The crucifixion of Jesus

John's account of the crucifixion, death and burial of Jesus is almost certainly an amalgam of three things: traditions shared with the other Gospels, historical memories recorded only in John, and later theological reflection. For example, Mark, Matthew and Luke say that Simon of Cyrene carried Jesus' cross (Mark 15.21; Matthew 27.32; Luke 23.26), whereas, according to John, Jesus carried his own cross. It is possible that all four evangelists are correct: Jesus carried his cross the first part of the way, and Simon the rest. Perhaps John is also making a theological statement about one who bears the sins of the world. John is alone in saying that the inscription over the cross, 'the king of the Jews', was written in three languages: Hebrew, Latin and Greek (19.20). Again, this may be both an authentic memory and a theological statement about the worldwide significance of what was happening.

Other details bring out its significance. Many commentators have noticed the similarity between John's description of Jesus' seamless robe (19.23) and the description of the high priest's robe given by the first-century Jewish historian Josephus; the words of Jesus to his mother and the Beloved Disciple spoke a new community into being (19.25–27; see Chapter 2); the Jesus who has promised that he will quench the thirst of all who come to him (compare 4.14; 6.35; 7.38) now bears the world's thirst (19.28); Jesus' final words, 'It is finished' (*tetelestai*, 19.30), recall the 'headline' of 13.2: 'Having loved his own who were in the world, he loved them to the end [*eis telos*].' There follows another example of the writer's studied ambiguity: the evangelist states that Jesus 'gave up his spirit', but a more literal translation would be that he 'handed over the Spirit' (19.30).[8] Finally, the burial of Jesus in John is carried out by two people, not one, as in the other Gospels. Here Nicodemus joins Joseph of Arimathea to anoint the body (v. 39). The extraordinary amount of 'myrrh and aloes' is a hundred times heavier and more expensive than the ointment Mary used (12.3). Josephus records that it took 500 servants to carry the spices for Herod's burial.[9] So, whatever originally happened, the writer wishes to portray a burial fit for a king.

So John's passion narrative is a rich tapestry of historical detail and theological commentary: an inspired, imaginative portrayal of a historical event at the very heart of Christian faith. And all of this, says the evangelist, in fulfilment of Scripture (for example 19.24, 37). That might sound like a contrived ordering of events to fit what had been prophesied. It would be more accurate to say that the testimony of all four Gospel writers to the fulfilment of Scripture in the crucifixion reflects their profound conviction that God was present in it all, working out his providential purpose.

The lifting up of the Son of Man

What does chapter 20 add to what John has so far narrated? That may seem a very strange question. Yet some years ago

---

8 As we noted in the discussion of this verse in Chapter 1, the Greek here does not have the word 'his', so what John actually wrote was 'Jesus . . . handed over *the* spirit'.

9 Andrew T. Lincoln, *The Gospel According to John*, London: Continuum, 2005, p. 485.

candidates in a theology examination were invited to discuss whether the resurrection narratives were essential to this Gospel. The short answer is: they are. But the question was inviting students to explore the extraordinary way in which this evangelist has turned the events of chapters 18 and 19 upside down. The trial of Jesus has become the trial of the world (12.31), exemplified especially in the conversation between Jesus and Pilate; the mockery of Jesus has become his coronation (19.1–14): 'Behold the man' (v. 5), 'Behold your king' (v. 14). Most of all, the lifting up of the Son of Man upon his cross is the hour of his glory (13.1; 17.1), his triumph (19.30) and the source of the world's salvation (3.14–15; 6.51). What more was there to say?

Mark wrote a Gospel without a resurrection appearance. Most scholars think that the last chapter of the Gospel of Mark originally ended at verse 8, with the promise to the women and, through them, to the disciples, that they would see the risen Jesus in Galilee (v. 7). So a Gospel without a resurrection appearance is not necessarily a contradiction in terms. So what do John's resurrection narratives add to what he has already said?

John, more than the other three evangelists, helps us to see that the resurrection *is* the meaning of the cross. That doesn't mean, of course, that it wasn't real. But John shows us that we cannot understand the resurrection without the cross – and vice versa. What is more, the resurrection cannot be reduced simply to a 'happy ever after' event. It carries within it the significance of the cross: the risen Jesus was recognized by his scars (20.20). The theological implications are profound.

Yet again, John gives us a picture that it would be a mistake to try to dissect, searching for historical details. The resurrection of Jesus, like the very existence of God, is the rock on which Christian faith stands. Neither the resurrection nor God's existence can be proved. But this detail of John's picture – that the risen Jesus was recognized by his wounds – takes us to the heart of the Christian understanding of God. The links between this final section of the Gospel (as it originally was), and preceding sections, particularly the farewell discourses, are important. The unusual reference to the cloth which 'had been on Jesus' head'

(20.7) recalls the headcloth (the same Greek word *soudarion*) of Lazarus (11.44); the personal address of the risen Jesus, 'Mary' (20.16) fulfils the promise that the Good Shepherd calls his sheep by name (10.3); and the gifts of peace, joy and the Holy Spirit bestowed by the risen Jesus on the disciples (20.19–23) fulfil the promises made in the farewell discourses (14.16, 27; 15.11; 16.22).

Finally, John, as clearly as Matthew and Luke but in his own distinctive way, testifies that, because of the resurrection, God's mission to the world goes on: 'As the Father has sent me, so I send you' (v. 21).[10]

In Chapter 5, particularly in the section entitled 'A Christlike God', we shall seek to draw out the theological implications of the transforming revelation as told by John in his Gospel.

---

10 The parallel here between Jesus and the disciples complements the parallels between the disciples and the Spirit in the last discourses: for example, they witness to Jesus, and so will the Spirit (15.26–27).

5

The Message of John's Gospel for Today

In my book *Paul for Today*[1] I pointed out that the New Testament carries a 'health warning' about the dangers of misinterpreting the letters of Paul (2 Peter 3.15–16). There is no such warning about reading the Gospel of John, and many Christians might be shocked at the very idea. Yet, as this book has tried to show, unwary readers might make 'the Jews' the scapegoats for the death of Jesus, or allow John's picture of Jesus, shaped as it is by later Christian conviction, to give them a skewed picture of how human he really was.

There may be a similar challenge in the Gospel's language about God. In reading the Bible, we are always prone to read preconceptions and ideas of our own into the text. So reading the Bible well involves a journey into a deeper self-knowledge which helps us to identify what we ourselves bring to the task. It is a lifetime's task, and we shall always 'see through a glass darkly' (1 Corinthians 13.12). By that I mean: we are bound to read the Bible through the lens of the particular person each of us is. This can make studying the Bible with people very different from ourselves both illuminating and valuable.

What has this to do with the Gospel of John's teaching about God? Simply this: all our preconceived ideas about God, including all that we've learned over the years, *whether they are right*

---

1 Neil Richardson, *Paul for Today: New Perspectives on a Controversial Apostle*, London: Epworth, 2009, p. ix.

or wrong, are likely to colour our reading of John. Are we really hearing what this Gospel is saying? Or are we reading into it ideas and concepts of God which are not there at all? We begin this chapter by seeking to relate this Gospel to the contemporary debate about God.

John and the contemporary debate about God

Dysfunctional religion

The twenty-first century has put God well and truly back in the headlines. The bombing of the twin towers in New York in 2001 by men who prayed as they did so has forced us all to recognize the connection between religion and violence. In fact, history down the centuries has been scarred by conflicts waged in the name of God, and around the world today there are wars and conflicts fuelled by religion: Northern Ireland, India, Pakistan and Iraq are just a few of the places affected by them.

If God exists, and if, as John's Gospel insists, God loves nothing less than the whole world, then any religion that fuels violence has to be labelled seriously dysfunctional. We see such religion quite often in TV fiction; I have lost count of the number of religious people – usually Christians, lay and ordained – who are portrayed as nasty, eccentric or sinister. While we are bound to acknowledge that, on the personal level as well as the international level, religion has done much harm, a Christian has to insist, in the light of Christ, that it is more important to be human than religious.[2]

Strident atheism

It is hardly surprising that a decade which has forced upon our attention the connection between religion and violence has

---

2 The New Testament's language about Jesus as God's Son, as the 'image of God' (for example 2 Corinthians 4.4), and its related language about Jesus as the 'last Adam' (for example 1 Corinthians 15.45, compare Romans 5.12–21) points to the conviction that Jesus reveals what it is to be fully and truly human.

produced a crop of strident atheists. I am not concerned here to refute their arguments; others, in my view, have done that effectively enough.[3] But those of us who hold to the Christian faith would do well to notice the element of truth in their criticisms. A form of religion that spawns violence or intolerance cannot be right. Religious zeal and moral indignation are dangerous and often destructive. If religious people themselves do not sufficiently recognize the dark side of religion, then someone needs to do so.

Yet Christians also need to say: we do not believe, either, in the god about whose character Richard Dawkins and others complain, and whose existence they deny. But it is a tragedy that Christians can be their own worst enemy. A clear example of this tragedy lies in the way in which many devout people seek to combat the teaching of evolution, and put it about that you cannot believe both in evolution and in a Creator God. How many thoughtful teenagers are turning away from Christian faith because they are being presented with these false alternatives?

So there are good reasons why Christians should think carefully and prayerfully about our inherited understanding of God, and our reading of the Bible. I incline to think that what a Benedictine writer wrote back in 1968 is as true now as it was then: 'What is most lacking today both in the world and in the Church . . . is an adequate concept of God.'[4]

Christian differences about God

Is it inevitable that Christians should hold different views about God? Yes, it is. A remarkable variety of beliefs about God can be found within the churches today, and it may be healthy. But

---

3 For example Alister McGrath and Joanna Collicutt McGrath, *The Dawkins Delusion: Atheist Fundamentalism and the Denial of the Divine*, London: SPCK, 2007.

4 Sebastian Moore, *God is a New Language*, London: Darton, Longman and Todd, 1967, p. 38.

it is not without its dangers. In our so-called post-modern age we tend to be more concerned with choice and values, rather than truth and absolutes. So it is easy to slide into a relativism which says, in effect, 'Well, you have your view of God, I have mine.'

But what if 'your' view, or 'mine', is seriously wrong? Who, if anybody, is to decide? One of the most crucial discussions we can have today concerns the nature and the centrality of love in Christian faith. Put at its simplest, the issue is this: is the statement 'God is love' (1 John 4.8, 16) the defining statement about the God revealed in Jesus? Or must it be placed alongside, and even qualified by, other statements about God? For example, is it correct to say not only 'God is love', *but also* (and the word 'but', if we use it here, is very revealing), 'God is holy', 'God is righteous' and so on? After all, these convictions are also reflected in the Bible.

I want to suggest that Christian thinking about God is often distorted by the belief that God's love must be 'balanced' by a sterner side to God, particularly his justice and his holiness. There is a healthy concern here to avoid the easy-going love of an indulgent parent. But if we reduce the divine love to just one attribute of God alongside other attributes which qualify that love, we have gone a long way towards losing the Gospel.

What I think happens is this. The sentence 'God is love' is so astonishingly simple and extraordinary that we cannot easily comprehend its awesome implications. Because so many of us have not been loved enough or, even if we have, still find it hard to love ourselves, we are likely to project on to God the conviction that a price has to be paid for our sin. In one sense, of course, that is true. Any person's wayward behaviour is deeply hurtful and distressing to those who love them; forgiveness is always costly. Yet this must not lead us to say, 'God loves us *but* his justice must be satisfed', or 'God is love, *but* God is holy as well'.

I do not wish to be misunderstood here. I am not saying that sin is not serious; God, by his very nature, does not and cannot compromise with sin (though *that* word, too, needs careful definition; what we think is sinful may not be sinful at all, or far less culpable than we imagine). But this must not lead us to suppose that God's justice and holiness have to be satisfied if God is ever to forgive our sin. Relationships – above all, relationships of love – simply do not work like that. A parable Jesus told (Luke 15.11–32) should be enough to persuade us of that; the parable also shows that suffering and sacrifice are always at the heart of reconciliation and forgiveness.

The result of our limited, perhaps guilt-ridden thinking is that we tend to alter, perhaps subconsciously, the belief that God is love into the belief 'there is a God who loves us, but . . .' The 'but' is a telling indication that we are qualifying God's love in a way that the New Testament does not.

'You do not know God': religion and the world in John

The world's ignorance of God

What does John's Gospel contribute to the contemporary debate about God? We begin with its negative message. It insists that 'the world' in its darkness and ignorance does not, and cannot know God. 'The world cannot receive' the Spirit of truth 'because it neither sees him nor knows him' (14.17). It would be a mistake to think that this verse refers only to the Holy Spirit, and not to God; if there is one thing above all else that the last discourses of John insist upon it is the inseparability of Spirit, Son and Father.

John's bleak assessment of the world's ignorance of God needs to be understood in the context of other biblical teaching about God. Paul at Athens says, God 'is not far from each one of us. "For in him we live and move and have our being"' (Acts 17.27–28; compare Romans 1.19–20). The prologue of John, in fact, with its assertion that 'he was in the world and the world came into being through him' (1.10), implies as much: the Creator is indeed present in his creation. But that verse from John must be heard in its entirety: 'yet the world did not know him'. Paul, in the Romans passage just cited, does not mince his words either: 'they are without excuse'. So the Bible testifies to the generous, invisible presence of God throughout his creation, *and* to humankind's refusal and failure (both, I think) to acknowledge God.

Leading characteristics of 'the world'

John's teaching about the world makes for searching reading. Just as we cannot identify 'the Jews' straightforwardly with a particular racial group, so we cannot simply contrast the Church and the world, as if they were two readily identifiable groups of people. True, the last discourses contrast the disciples with the world. But the world in John is identifiable by certain characteristics; it is these that define 'the world' (see the conclusion in Chapter 3).

The Gospel of John repeatedly insists that the world's deeds are evil (3.19; 7.7; 15.18, 22). If 'the world' were to mean 'the whole creation and everyone in it', that would clearly not be true. Goodness will keep on breaking out as well, often in surprising places. Yet we mustn't understate the seriousness of what John is saying either. Creation as a whole is 'off-centre' and, *as a world gone wrong*, its deeds are bound to exemplify that wrongness. The reason why it hates Jesus is because he exposed its sinfulness. Yet this Gospel also asserts that Jesus came to save the world, not to condemn it (3.17; 12.47). How is this apparent contradiction to be explained? The answer lies in some teaching of Jesus in John 8: 'You judge by human standards; I judge no one. Yet even if I do judge, my judgement is valid, for it is not I alone who judge, but I and the Father who sent me' (vv. 15–16).

So Jesus, precisely by *not* judging anyone, puts the whole world in the wrong, because that is what all of us do most of the time. We can't help it; it comes naturally to us. As the philosopher Thomas Hobbes said, 'A man's chief joy consists in comparing himself with others.' But, as the Gospel implies, our judgements are often superficial and wrong. (We judge 'by human standards'.) Newspaper headlines most days of the week illustrate the point well. We go in for scapegoating individuals, groups, governments; we find it hard to see other people and ourselves clearly (Matthew 7.1–5). That is not all. We are not very good at hating the sin and loving the sinner. We usually lump the two together, and roundly condemn both. (The story of the woman taken in adultery – John 7.53 – 8.11 – provides both an illustration and a powerful contrast.)

So judging 'by human standards' is one characteristic of the world. There is another striking contrast between Jesus and 'the world'. Jesus seeks the glory of the One who sent him (7.18), not his own glory (8.50, 54). By contrast, everyone else accepts glory from each other (5.44). The word 'glory' (*doxa*) means the intrinsic honour and worth of a person; but is that to be discovered and determined solely through competition with others, or by the say-so of others? That is how 'the world' usually works. As with judging, we may say that is surely natural. But Scripture urges on us something deeper and infinitely more worthwhile. The glory of God is what matters, not the glory which comes from other people (5.44; 12.43).

This might suggest that God is at the top of a cosmic pyramid, a sort of celestial emperor to whom all his subjects are supposed to give glory. But here is a most extraordinary contrast with the world's self-seeking. God gives his glory away – first, to his son Jesus, and then, through Jesus, to everyone else – or potentially everyone else (17.1, 22). We shall return to this remarkable theme in the next section. But for now we note this second characteristic of the world, in contrast to Jesus: people seek glory from each other.

This Gospel also insists that Jesus cannot reveal himself to the world. The brothers of Jesus urge on Jesus the necessity of some publicity for himself (7.4). The evangelist attributes this mistaken advice to their unbelief (v. 5). Jesus responds that the world hates him (v. 7). Is that not all the more reason for Jesus doing something about it? It would seem so. Instead Jesus talks mysteriously about his 'time' (v. 8). A disciple ('Judas, not Iscariot') later enquires how it is that Jesus will reveal himself to the disciples but not to the world (14.22). Jesus seems not to reply at all, almost repeating what he has just said: 'Jesus answered him, "Those who love me will keep my word, and my Father will love them, and we will come to them and make our home with them"' (v. 23; compare v. 21). This 'coming', this revelation, is the only revelation there will be: the God who sent Jesus, by touching hearts and minds, heals and transforms human lives. So there cannot be a revelation to the world as the world. That would be a contradiction in terms. 'The world' in John is, for the most part, not a neutral, descriptive word, but a theologically loaded one – like Paul's word 'flesh'. It means not simply 'the world', but 'the world-gone-wrong', and that is why, as the world, it *cannot* receive God's revelation. But, rather than engaging in a display of celestial pyrotechnics which browbeats the world into belief, the God who sent Jesus works in a different way.

John's Gospel and religion's ignorance of God

Not only does 'the world' not know the God who sent Jesus, but many religious people do not know God either. That is the clear conclusion to be drawn from the Gospel's portrayal of 'the Jews' and 'the Pharisees' (for example 7.28; 8.55). But here, too, we cannot simply identify 'the Jews' as a group racially and historically distinct from ourselves (Chapter 3). Rather, we must ask, as we did with 'the world', what are the characteristics of those people whom John calls 'the Jews'. The label is Jewish, but it is the characteristics which matter, and 'if the cap fits . . .'.

There are hints, and more than hints, that many religious people should know what they do not know. Jesus answered Nicodemus with a counter-question, 'Are you a teacher of Israel, and yet you do not understand these things?' (3.10). Later, he points out to 'the Jews' that their Scriptures testify to him (5.39).

There are other negative characteristics. But their fundamental failure is the failure to recognize and acknowledge Jesus. Does this not exonerate Christians who, after all, may be defined as the people who *do* acknowledge Jesus? But then the question must be pressed: how deep does such acknowledgement go? 'Not everyone who says to me, "Lord, Lord", will enter the kingdom of heaven' (Matthew 7.21; compare the 'parable' of the sheep and the goats in Matthew 25, especially vv. 44–45).

The parable of the sheep and the goats helps to remind us of another way in which religion can betray its ignorance of God. It bypasses or ostracizes the stranger, the lame and the blind

(4.27; 5.2–4; 9.1), or tells them it's their fault (9.2); it mercilessly punishes the sinner (8.4–5); it well and truly buries the dead (11.38–39). These themes are more prominent in the other Gospels, but they are here in John as well.

What religion and the world have in common

It would be a mistake to distinguish too sharply between the religious and the worldly opposition to Jesus. Although earlier I described 'seeking glory from each other' as a characteristic of 'the world', it is an accusation which Jesus makes against 'the Jews'. But that is the point. Similarly, 'the world', despite some honourable exceptions, does no better than religion in its care of the marginalized. Each generation, each society creates its own scapegoats and marginalized groups.

There is another characteristic that religion and 'the world' have in common: they both persecute (15.18–21; 16.1–3). They are indistinguishable in their hatred of the Father and the Son (15.24). Why do they hate Jesus? Jesus says here that they hate 'without cause' (v. 27), an echo of the Psalms (35.19; 69.5). This must mean 'without *good* cause', because the context shows there is a cause. They hate Jesus because he has exposed their sin by what he said (v. 22; compare 3.19; 7.7; 16.8–11), and by what he did (v. 24), including deeds 'which no else did'.

What are these deeds of Jesus? The Gospel itself tells us: turning water into wine, healing the sick, befriending the stranger, feeding the hungry, enabling the lame to walk, the blind to see and the dead to live. What Jesus did still stands in stark contrast with the failures of religion and the world. How anyone responds to the equivalent groups in their own day is an acid test of whether they 'believe'.

How else are we to determine whether anyone, including ourselves, knows God? We would be wise, of course, to confine the enquiry to ourselves. In an earlier book, I suggested that 'whatever a person worships shapes that person's life in certain ways. What a person worships may sometimes be deduced from the imprint of that reality (even if that reality is an idol), upon that person's life.' '. . . according to the New Testament, it is Christ who offers the clearest, fullest picture of the divine imprint on a human life', and therefore the imprint on human life of the God of Jesus is characterized, above all, by faith, love and hope.[5]

With this in mind, we continue our exploration of John's message for today by looking once more at the central figure of that Gospel.

A Christlike God

If, as we have seen, religion can be dysfunctional and the world unheeding of and hostile to God, what is the fundamental message of John's Gospel? As we have seen, it is bleakly realistic in its portrayal of the response to Jesus of both religion and the world. We begin our exploration in this section from the fact that the Gospel of John is both God-centred and Jesus-centred, and we ask: what are the fundamental themes and convictions behind this predominant characteristic of the Gospel, and their theological implications for us today?

A Jesus-centred faith?

Some contemporary expressions of Christianity are very Jesus-centred – sometimes to the exclusion of God. Some people are attracted by the moral example of Jesus and by the teaching of the Gospels, particularly the Sermon on the Mount. They may be quite uncertain or even unconcerned about the relationship of Jesus and his teaching to God. Sometimes contemporary worship is very Jesus-centred. I recall attending a service of worship in which the worship and songs were focused exclusively on Jesus, and God was hardly mentioned in the service at all. We shall note later in this chapter that the opposite can happen: expressions of so-called Christian faith focus on God and marginalize

---

5 Neil Richardson, *God in the New Testament*, Peterborough: Epworth, 1999, pp. 10 and 99–103.

Jesus. But John's Gospel seems to beckon us in the direction of a faith that is both God-centred and Jesus-centred, centring our lives on a Christlike God. In exploring this theme, we look first at what the Church has traditionally called the divinity of Jesus.

Orthodoxy and heresy

At a conference a few years ago, a member of the same working group as myself expressed horror on one occasion at something I had said. I had used the word 'orthodox' – a word which, for her, was full of oppressive, negative connotations. I should not have been surprised at her reaction. For some 'orthodox' is a positive word: literally, it means 'the right way'. But what if 'the right way' looks narrow, or what if 'orthodoxy' has been used as a threat to browbeat others into line?

Whatever our personal reaction to the word, orthodox Christian belief about Jesus has not been in doubt for many centuries now. People may disagree with it; Christians themselves may differ about the interpretation of it, but as we noted in the previous chapter, Christian faith has maintained, explicitly since the fifth century, and implicitly long before that, that Jesus was fully human and fully divine.

It is likely that John's community took for granted the humanity of Jesus. If the tradition about John is correct, then eyewitness experience lies behind the resounding testimony with which the First Letter of John begins: 'We declare to you what was from the beginning, what we have heard, what we have seen with our eyes, what we have looked at and touched with our hands, concerning the word of life' (1 John 1.1). Here, however, we focus our attention on the divinity of Jesus. 'Divinity' is a word easily misunderstood, and not a word used by John, and so we would do better to concentrate on what John actually says, rather than flatten it all out into the abstract concept of later creeds. The basic themes in John are simple, and are replayed over and over: God sent Jesus; God and Jesus were Father and Son, Jesus returned to God, and Jesus is the One ('I am . . .'). We shall need to unpack each of these themes a little more.

God sent Jesus

God also sent Amos, Isaiah and all the other prophets. But the Gospel means far more. This is why the question of where Jesus is *from* crops up again and again. Unlike Amos and the rest, the life of 'the Son' did not begin on earth, but in heaven. (Even to say 'began' is misleading, since there are no beginnings and endings in eternity.) Amos, unlike 'the Son of Man', did not descend from heaven (3.13; 6.33, 38, etc.). In this Gospel leading figures of the Scriptures testify to Jesus: Isaiah, for example, saw the glory of the Son (12.41), a glory shared with the Father before the world was (17.5).

It is as well to recognize that we are out of our depth with language like this. We need to avoid saying '*Jesus* was in heaven before he came to earth', since the life of Jesus began with his birth in 4 BC, or whenever it was. But we also need to consult our trusty 'programme notes': 'in the beginning was the Word', and that Word is to be both distinguished from God and yet identified with him (1.1), just as the body of the Gospel will distinguish between the Father and the Son, and yet insist on their equality and their perfect unity: 'My Father is still working, and I also am working' (5.17) and 'the Father and I are one' (10.30).

So this is the first of John's key points about 'the divinity' of Jesus: God sent his Son – from heaven, and 'the Word became flesh'. To put it over-colloquially, Father and Son go back a long way together – as far as eternity. Paul, at an earlier stage of Christian reflection, is on the same trajectory in his reference to 'one God' and 'one Lord' (1 Corinthians 8.6).

Father and Son

There is a lot of Father–Son language in John, but two main themes can be seen. The Son is utterly open to the Father, dependent upon him, obedient to him. He says and does nothing which does not have the divine imprimatur upon it. That is his mission. If we were using the language of the other Gospels, we might say that 'the Kingdom of God' was the all-embracing reality which governed Jesus' life.

The other main theme of John's Father–Son language arises from the first. Because Jesus is so utterly transparent to God, to the eyes of faith the divine glory shines through in full, transforming force – even, or rather, above all, on the cross (2.11; 13.31–32; 17.1). This is why there are so many Father–Son parallels in John: 'he who has seen me has seen the Father' (14.9; see Chapter 4).

The Old Testament has language rather like this. It talks of God's Wisdom and God's Spirit. Neither the divine Wisdom nor the divine Spirit were less than God – as if substitutes for the real thing – still less were they messengers from heaven, like angels. Yet we need also to say: God isn't *only* his Wisdom, *only* his Spirit. In a similar way, John's Gospel seems to say: to do justice to the mystery of God, you need to say, not only 'Father' but 'Son', not only 'Son', but also 'Father'. Indeed, you cannot say one without the other. And as we saw, the farewell discourses of Jesus in this Gospel more than hint that a third 'person' is also needed to do justice to God.

The return to the Father

The twin questions of where Jesus is from, and where he is going, frame John's Gospel. After the summary which concludes the first part of the Gospel (12.44–50), the second and final part opens with a recapitulation of some major themes: 'And during supper Jesus, knowing that the Father had given all things into his hands, and that he had come from God and was going to God . . .' (13.3). Jesus first speaks of his departure to 'the Jews' (7.33; 8.14, 21), and later to his disciples, when it becomes clear where he was going – to the Father (14.4–5; 16.5; 10.17). What he has foretold again and again finally comes to pass in what reads very much like John's version of the ascension, 'I am ascending to my Father and your Father, to my God and your God' (20.17; on this verse, see also Chapter 3).

This theme of the return to the Father is an especially important example of what I have called John carrying on where the other Gospels leave off, or of John making more explicit what the others merely hint at, or imply. The Son's return to the Father is what the resurrection meant and continues to mean. And the Son's return to the Father means that others may now share in the divine life: God has, as it were, extended himself to embrace us all: 'as you Father are in me and I am in you, may they also be in us, so that the world may believe that you have sent me' (17.21).

The unselfishness of God

John's language about the Father and the Son points up the utter selflessness of God. 'The Father loves the Son and has placed all things in his hands' (3.35), and the Son is equally unselfish, seeking not his own glory (8.50). The cross is the supreme revelation of this divine unselfishness. In the other Gospels we are told of the divine voice at the baptism and transfiguration of Jesus saying, 'This is my Son'. The cross is the climax of this self-effacement of the Father as, in the profound paradox of a crucifixion, he glorifies the Son. The crucifixion is also the climax of the Son's obedience.

This mutual self-effacement of the Father and the Son lies behind the words uttered by Jesus after the exit of Judas in the darkness of 'the night' (13.30): 'When he had gone out, Jesus said, "Now the Son of Man has been glorified, and God has been glorified in him. If God has been glorified in him, God will also glorify him in himself and will glorify him at once"' (13.31–32).

So there is a 'partnership' of love between the Father and the Son. The Father entrusts everything to the Son, the Son wholeheartedly obeys the Father, and each 'glorifies' the other.

I am the One

We come to the last of John's fundamental points about Jesus. It arises from the other three. Because Jesus was truly 'one of us' (though that is the language of Hebrews, rather than of John – for example Hebrews 2.11–12; 4.15), and because he was the Father's 'one and only' Son (John 1.18), coming from and returning to God, Jesus is the One who becomes our life. This theme is developed throughout the Gospel, but finds its most concentrated expressions in the so-called 'I am' sayings.

The 'I am' sayings of John's Gospel fall into two groups. The better-known group consists basically of 7 sayings, though several of these are repeated. They are:

- 'I am the bread of life.' (6.35, 48, though vv. 41 and 51 also have 'I am')
- 'I am the light of the world.' (8.12; 9.5)
- 'I am the door' (of the sheep). (10.7, 9)
- 'I am the good shepherd.' (10.11,14)
- 'I am the resurrection and the life.' (11.25)
- 'I am the way and the truth and the life.' (14.6)
- 'I am the true vine.' (15.1, compare v. 5)[6]

But there is another group of sayings attributed to Jesus in John in which the same two Greek words *ego eimi* (literally, 'I am') occur. There are several of these, and in places, such as John 6.20, we can translate the words simply as 'It's me'. Here Jesus is re-assuring his terrified disciples as they cross the Sea of Galilee. So, in Jesus' reply to 'the Jews' at 8.28, he says: 'When you have lifted up the Son of Man, then you will realize that I am he' (*ego eimi*, NRSV translation). The same two Greek words occur at the end of this chapter: 'before Abraham was, I am' (v. 58 NRSV translation).

It's worth looking more closely at the Old Testament background. People often point to Exodus 3.14, where God reveals his name to Moses: 'I am who I am' (Greek, *ego eimi ho on*). But there is another section of the Old Testament, Isaiah 40–55, which is relevant here. And here the same two Greek words occur, even, in some verses, being repeated. So where the NRSV translates 'I, I am he', the repeated pronoun is meant to reflect the repetition in both the Greek (and Hebrew): *ego eimi, ego*

---

6 Taken from Barrett, *Regospel According to St John*, p. 242; Barrett also includes 8.18 and 23 in his list, two verses which have the Greek words *ego eimi* without a predicate. (See the NRSV footnotes here.)

eimi (Isaiah 43.25 is one such example). (There are also examples in the wider Greek and Roman world of gods and goddesses announcing their presence: 'I am . . .'.)

The 'I am' sayings, and their Old Testament background, not forgetting Greek and Roman parallels, are surely intended to be a revelation of the divinity of Jesus. However, not all scholars think that the 'I am' sayings of Jesus express his divinity. They translate John 6.35, for example, as 'The bread of life: it is I.' So the emphasis falls on the bread, and where it is to be found – that is in Jesus. But even with this different emphasis the implication of Jesus' divinity seems to me unmistakable. 'Divinity', however, is an abstract, even cold word, and does not help us in appreciating the attractiveness of John's Gospel. It is far better to think of the 'I am' sayings as indicating all that God is, and wants to be, to be to the world he has made: its light, its way, its truth, its deepest, fullest life, the one who satisfies its deepest hunger and thirst.

The Gospel's beginning and end

So many recurring themes and phrases in this Gospel direct us towards the 'divinity' of Jesus: God sent him from heaven, the Father and the Son are one, Jesus returns to God and, fourth, as we have just seen, the recurring expression 'I am' also underscores what the prologue flagged up: the Word who is God (1.1) was made flesh (1.14).

Two more verses in John are extremely important in this context. The last verse of the prologue (1.18) is a place in the New Testament where our oldest manuscripts are intriguingly different. Did John write 'the only begotten Son' has made God known, or 'the only begotten God'? In instances like these, scholars tend to ask: which of these two expressions are later Christian scribes more likely to have altered? In other words, the more difficult version is more likely to be the original one – otherwise, it wouldn't have been altered.[7] Here the answer is not clear-cut at

---

7 The REB follows the more difficult reading at Mark 1.40, translating 'Jesus was moved to anger'. The translators here clearly concluded that Mark is more

all. But, whichever expression John originally wrote, it reinforces the emphasis of earlier verses (1.1, 14) that the Son whose mission is now to be recounted is, in Matthew's expression (Matthew 1.23), God with us.

The other verse comes almost at what was the Gospel's original ending (20.28). The story of Thomas (20.24–29) does not feature in the other Gospels, but it brings together the twin emphases of the prologue. Its emphasis on the wounds of Jesus (v. 25) takes us back to the incarnate Word (1.14), while the confession of Thomas, 'My Lord and my God', brings us full circle to the Jesus who is God with us and God for us. In the rest of this section we shall seek to draw out some contemporary theological implications of this claim. Before we do so, one further question needs to be asked: in the view of this Gospel writer was Jesus' death on the cross necessary?

John's teaching on the cross

The teaching of John's Gospel about the death of Jesus is allusive, yet powerful. References to the Passover run through this Gospel (from 2.13 to 19.14); 19.14 hints that Jesus himself is the Passover lamb. Although the Passover meal in Jewish tradition was not a sacrifice for sin, an early notice in this Gospel seems to combine different strands of the Old Testament's teaching on sacrifice: 'Here is the Lamb of God who takes away the sin of the world!' (1.29). The long discourse on bread in chapter 6 reinforces the sacrificial theme: 'the bread that I will give for the life of the world is my flesh'. The evangelist repeats and develops this theme many times: the Good Shepherd gives his life for the sheep, Jesus' washing of his disciples' feet enacts, in a parable-like action, his sacrificial death (13.1–15), a man gives his life for his friends (15.13). Several of the distinctive features of John's passion narrative, as we saw in the previous chapter, subtly highlight the significance of the cross.

---

likely to have written the Greek 'moved to anger' (*orgistheis*), than the more obvious 'moved with compassion' (*splanchnistheis*).

So, while we cannot attribute to John a theory of what the Church came to call the atonement, many details serve to highlight the sacrificial nature of Jesus' death. And all of this needs to be placed in the framework of the extraordinary way in which this Gospel wants us to see the crucifixion (of all things) as his exaltation: 'the Son of Man must be lifted up' (3.13–14; 12.32–33). And, in all of this, the Father glorifies the Son, in order that the Son might glorify the Father (17.1, compare 13.31–32).

The glory of God

Whole books have been written on the subject of a 'Christlike' God.[8] Our concern here is to draw out one way in which John's Gospel invites us to see the glory of God in the light of Christ, and particularly his cross. Traditional Christian language and imagery do not always help here. 'Jesus, high in glory' was one of the first hymns I ever sang as a child. It is not a helpful introduction to John's Gospel. What our contemporary culture calls 'glory' helps even less. Glory is associated with success in sport, or heroic achievements on the field of battle. The ancient world's 'take' on glory was not so different from ours. In cultures dominated by honour, status and wealth, people prized and relished whatever glory they might win in order to impress their contemporaries. Solomon's glory was proverbial (Matthew 6.29; Luke 12.27).

So what was God's glory? In the Old Testament the divine honour and glory were so closely associated as to be virtually identical, and on the threshold of the New Testament era, many people, with varying hopes and expectations, awaited a revelation of the divine glory. In the other Gospels, the word 'glory' is rare; in the picture they give us of the life and death of Jesus, it's as if the divine glory shines through only in very special moments: his birth (for example Luke 2.9), his baptism and his transfiguration. With John it is different; as often he makes more explicit what the earlier Gospels merely hint at: 'we saw his glory' – all the way through his life, and even in his death (for example 1.14; 2.11; 17.1).

---

8 Notably John V. Taylor, *The Christlike God*, London: SCM, 1992.

But it is the definition of God's glory in the prologue that really gives John's 'angle' on God's glory its distinctiveness. Crucially, the evangelist tells his readers that the glory of the Word made flesh is 'the glory as of a father's only son, full of grace and truth' (1.14). 'Grace and truth' recall what the Old Testament says about God (for example Exodus 34.6): they can be paraphrased as 'God's undeserved favour and faithfulness to his own character'.[9] As always, what the Gospel's prologue says governs all that follows. This is what John means when he writes about the glory of the Father and the Son (the same glory): God's undeserved favour and faithfulness. Most significant of all, the crucifixion is the epicentre of the revelation of that glory.

A conclusion

Many people, both in the churches and beyond them, find language about the divinity of Jesus and God as a 'Holy Trinity' difficult. Is it really necessary? Many have a sneaking suspicion that the doctrine of the Trinity is an unnecessary complication to what should be a simpler faith. But John's Gospel, and the first letter which bears his name, can, I believe, help us see that the later doctrine of the Trinity, including belief in the divinity of 'the Son', is simply the working out of what the New Testament declares: 'God is love' (1 John 4.8, 16). The Gospel's story of a mission declares the story of an outgoing God who, in his selflessness, did not keep himself to himself, but made a world. The 'coming' of Jesus tells us more: this selfless God gave and gives himself for the world he is making.

John is a long way from using the later language of the Church about the Trinity. But I suggest that there is a slow, gradual transition from John to later orthodoxy. The golden thread that links the two is, quite simply, divine love. One of the greatest theologians of the twentieth century, Wolfhart Pannenberg, ends his three-volume *Systematic Theology* with these words: 'The . . . unity . . .

9 C. K. Barrett, *The Gospel According to St. John*, London: SPCK, 1955, p.139

of the Trinity constitutes the heartbeat of divine love, and with a single such heartbeat this love encompasses the whole world.'[10]

A Church that believes?

In an earlier section we noted the negative portrayal in this Gospel of both religion and the world. While we need resolutely to avoid pointing the finger at any group of people, the Gospel bluntly states that 'the Jews' and 'the world' do not know God. We may conclude from this that neither religion (as portrayed here) nor 'the world' can satisfy the deepest hunger and thirst of humankind. However hard they try – and religious and secular attempts to do so are many – they fail, or their success is temporary.

By contrast, there is no escaping the huge claims John's Gospel makes for Jesus: who he is in relation to God, and what he is in relation to humankind (the bread of life, the way, etc.). So *through him* people – all people – may come to know God. But how? The Gospel's insistent answer is: *by believing.*

The call to believe

The evangelist uses this word as if its meaning is self-evident: 'believe in', 'believe that', simply 'believe'. But believing is precisely what so many people today – inside and outside the churches – find problematical and difficult. What does it mean? And what are we to make of the Gospel's recurring refrain that we can't make ourselves believe, only God can do that (for example 6.44)?

That is one of the Gospel's dominant themes. But the Gospel also implies human responsibility. Negatively, the world's culpability consists in preferring darkness to light (3.19). But positively, people can take first steps: 'Come, and you will see,' says Jesus to the first disciples (1.39); 'Follow me' (to Philip, 1.43), 'Search the Scriptures' (to 'the Jews' 5.40). In fact, the prologue combines the divine initiative in making disciples with human response: such

10 W. Pannenberg, *Systematic Theology*, vol. 3, Edinburgh: T. & T. Clark, 1998, p. 646.

disciples are not 'born . . . of the will of man, but of God', but this is said of 'all who received him' (1.12–13). But ultimately all these roads – coming, following, searching, receiving – merge into one: 'Jesus answered them, "This is the work of God, that you believe in him whom he has sent"' (6.29).

John's Gospel shows that there are different 'levels' of believing. For example many 'Jews' believed in Jesus (8.30), but the sequel shows that their belief did not go very deep. The puzzled question of Judas ('not Iscariot') about why Jesus is revealing himself to disciples only, and not to the world (14.22), suggests that he, too, still has some way to go. Fundamentally, however, believing in Jesus means believing that he is the Christ, the Son of God (20.30–31), that he came from God and returned to God , and that Father and Son are one – not just of one mind or similar, but one in that each indwells the other. In other words, to believe in Jesus is to believe that Jesus was, is and always will be God's supreme expression of himself in human life *and* – a critical addition, this – to give him the allegiance of one's life and heart. All this is implied in the prologue's phrase 'believe in his name' (1.12).

This seems alarmingly like the reference in Lewis Carroll's *Alice* of believing six impossible things before breakfast. It is not surprising that this Gospel insists that we can't simply make ourselves believers. That, of itself, would be cause for despair, but we must not lose sight of its conviction that God loves *the world*, and of its hope that the world may come to believe (17.21, 23, compare 12.32).

So what is this Gospel saying to the churches today? There is a challenge to them *to believe*, rather than merely be religious. Just as Christian faith can be so Jesus-centred as to marginalize God (see the previous section), so the opposite can happen: so-called 'Christian' faith can degenerate into a vague belief in God hardly affected or shaped by the revelation which came through Jesus Christ. What this Gospel says so clearly is that revelation by definition is *transforming*. Belief which is not life-transforming is not really belief at all. Belief in God, in the way in which this Gospel understands it, is an intensely practical affair. Other New Testament writers labour the same point: we may say we believe in God, but our lives are the real proof – or disproof – of whether we believe or not.

Perhaps the greatest challenge of this Gospel to the churches today is to keep on recentring their life and worship in the transforming reality of the Spirit, Son and Father ('abide in me' (15.4)). But we can be more specific. Two themes, in particular, from the prayer of Jesus in John 17, deserve exploration.

What Jesus wanted most for his Church

On the evidence of the Gospels, it is difficult to deny that what Jesus wanted most for his Church is its unity. Three times in John Jesus prays that his disciples may be one (17.11; 21.22–23). But what kind of unity? In John's Gospel, such unity is always linked with the unity of the Father and the Son: 'may they be one as we are one' (17.11, 22). About this divine unity, the Gospel says many things: for example, the Father and the Son are united in mission to save the world, and the glory of the Son is the glory of the Father, and vice versa. Above all, it is the unity of love, the root of which is a mutual 'indwelling' ('I in you and you in me'). Into this unity, as we have seen, disciples are drawn (14.23; 15.5, etc.).

So the unity for which Jesus prays is a spiritual unity, rooted in the disciples' shared relationship with Jesus and with God. Does this mean that modern attempts to achieve Christian unity are misguided and shallow by comparison? They could be, but they need not be.

The message of John to the Church today, particularly in the so-called developed world, is one of *depth*: a call to live from the centre. This is how a remarkable Quaker of the twentieth century, in a book which has become a devotional classic, describes the experience:

The final grounds of holy Fellowship are in God. Lives immersed and drowned in God are drowned in love, and know one another in Him, and know one another in love. Such lives have a common meeting-point. They go back to a single Centre where they are at home with Him and with one another. It is as if every soul had a final base, and that final base of every soul is one single Holy Ground, shared in by all. Persons in the Fellowship are related to one another through Him, as all mountains go down into the same earth.[11]

A glory shared

A closely related theme also enunciated in the same prayer is the gift from Jesus to the disciples of the divine glory: 'The glory that you have given me I have given them so that they may be one, as we are one' (17.22). Once again, Christian tradition has sometimes obscured the striking character of this gift. A large church or cathedral built 'to the glory of God' might suggest that glory has something to do with size or grandeur. But our earlier discussion showed what this Gospel understands by the glory of God: God's undeserved love and faithfulness, reflected in the Church's own generous love to others. This is what spills over on to the Church. It is no accident that the glory and unity of the Church are so closely related; both are rooted in the Love which is the foundation of the Church.

So the true glory of the Church is not to be found in large congregations and impressive buildings, or even in mass conversions. It *may* be seen in such things. But this Gospel guides us to a different criterion: the Church's glory is revealed most of all in the sacrificial self-giving which finds its pattern, inspiration and, ultimately, its power, in the cross. A man who exercised a costly, sacrificial ministry as a chaplain to soldiers in the trenches of the First World War expresses it well in a poem with the John-like title 'High and Lifted Up':

Thou hast bid us seek Thy glory, in a criminal crucified.
And we find it – for Thy glory is the glory of Love's loss,
And Thou hast no other splendour but the splendour of the
    Cross.[12]

---

11 Thomas Kelly, *A Testament of Devotion*, London: Hodder and Stoughton, 1941, p. 76.

12 G. A. Studdert Kennedy, *The Unutterable Beauty*, London: Hodder and Stoughton, 1927, p. 37.

Many pressures today conspire to make church life and worship shallow and superficial. They do not need to be rehearsed here. John's Gospel calls the Church to live from the centre; unless it does so, it withers and dies (John 15.6). From that centre, the Church is called to live at the heart of the world. That is the real test of the reality and depth of its belief in Jesus. With that in mind, we turn once more to the theme of God's mission to the world.

God's mission to the world

Where in the world?

When the Church does not live from its true centre – life in the Spirit, Son and Father (to keep John's language for this 'centre') – two things tend to happen. The Church loses its cutting-edge over against 'the world': it ceases to be prophetic and counter-cultural. (Its prophetic ministry cannot be measured simply by the extent to which the Church condemns the world but, rather, by 'doing the truth', 3.21.) The Church, or any local church, can sleepwalk into this atrophied state by absorbing, however unknowingly, the values and mores of the culture and society in which it is set. Such values and mores are never wholly wrong – far from it; they are usually a thorough mix of good and bad. But that is the point. A church that ceases to live from the centre will no longer be sufficiently discerning or alert to discriminate between the good, the bad and the indifferent.

But something else happens to a church no longer living from its centre. It ceases to be immersed effectively in the world. That may seem to contradict what I have just written. But, as I argued in an earlier chapter (Chapter 3), the closer a person draws to God, the more immersed they will be in the life of the world; or, to make the point more precisely, the more involved they will be in God's mission to the world.

In short, a church which is neither counter-cultural nor involved in mission to the world is likely to create its own culture and become a religious ghetto. In practice, the situation of most churches is more complex: we live partly or intermittently from our true centre. But that is the perennial challenge of John's Gospel: to live permanently and completely from that centre.

A *world-affirming and world-denying Gospel*

What other perspectives on the world does John give us? First, a church faithful to this Gospel will be both world-affirming and world-denying. John has far more negatives than positives about the world; that arose, no doubt, from his context. But that must not lead us to get the balance wrong. The positives are only two in number, but they are crucial: God made the world, and God loves it (John 1.3–4, 10; 3.16). And the negatives, many though they are, do not cancel out these fundamental truths: 'The light shines in the darkness, and the darkness has not overcome it' (1.5). If it had, there wouldn't be a Gospel of John at all nor any other Gospel.

But we must explore these themes a little more, if we are to try to do justice to the attractiveness of John's Gospel. To be world-affirming is to recognize and to celebrate all that God richly gives 'for our enjoyment' (1 Timothy 6.17). Admittedly, those words come from a letter attributed to Paul, but they are expressed elsewhere in the Bible (notably in Psalm 104), and they are implied by John's affirmation that 'all things were made by him'.

Why is it that the churches, or Christians in general, are sometimes slow, or reluctant, to affirm the goodness and the good things of the world around us? Maybe we are a little nervous of 'the world out there': but as another 'John' in the New Testament tells us, 'perfect love casts out fear' (1 John 4.18). The more the Church lives from its centre, the less fearful it will be.

Most fundamental of all – and this is the second of John's positives – God loves the world. That central mystery of Christian faith is the guiding light for Christian attitudes to the world. We must return to that later. But that does not cancel out the vocation of the Church to be world-denying, as well as world-affirming. 'World-denying' is easily misconstrued, especially by a Church nervous or judgemental of the world around. But if the earlier discussion in this chapter about religion and the world was on the right lines, then a believing, world-denying Church will be characterized by two things above all: its unity in the unity of the Father and the Son, and its renunciation of self-seeking as it reflects the divine glory revealed in the cross. This unity and selflessness will stand in gentle, but powerful contrast to a fragmented, self-seeking 'world'.

The fundamental challenge to the Church is presented starkly: out of what centre will we live? Will we live from (or in) our true centre, or from those values, lies and half-truths – including its mistaken judgements and glory-seeking – which comprise 'the world'?

Is John optimistic or pessimistic about the world?

This is a natural question for us to ask in the twenty-first century, when there are greater question marks over the future of our world than ever before. But we need to set aside the words 'optimism' and 'pessimism', which are attitudes based on our temperament, or our circumstances, or a mixture of the two. In their place we need to put two others, both of which are part of the perspective of this Gospel on the world. The first word is 'realism'.

John has no illusions about the world; it ostracizes its own Creator (1.11–12), preferring darkness to light because its deeds are evil (3.19). For people who live in a tolerant liberal democracy, this language may well sound extreme and even unfair. But we need to stay with John's language. The charge is that we (the human race) prefer shadows, illusions and self-deceptions (darkness) to truth. In this respect no country, no society has a clean sheet.

In a powerful sermon preached some years ago before the University of Oxford, the theologian Nicholas Lash took as his starting-point some words of Bonhoeffer's: 'Reality lays itself bare.' But he went on to say that our capacity for deceiving ourselves and the clouding of our moral vision leads us into some fundamental self-deceptions. He listed our reliance on nuclear deterrents, the effects of our policies – financial, economic and political – on 'the South', and 'the alienation, destitution and social instability' of our own society.[13] A quarter of a century later, similar charges could be made, with the additional charge of environmental destruction: we still prefer the darkness of illusions and self-deceptions, although there are occasional glimmers of the light of realism and truth.

Fortunately, another word is needed, alongside 'realism', to do justice to John's perspective on the world. This second word is 'hope'. The word itself does not occur in John, but hopefulness springs from the Gospel's fundamental convictions: God made the world, God loves it, and the light of God's love shines on in the darkness. That is our hope.

Will God intervene?

What answer to this question does John seem to give? We have already noted that there is little or nothing in this Gospel about the second coming of Christ. The other Gospels envisage the Son of Man coming with the clouds of heaven (Mark 14.62), and the Acts of the Apostles holds out the hope that Jesus will come in the same way as he ascended into heaven (Acts 1.11). But we have to ask whether this is to be understood literally or in some other way. (We should consider whether the biblical writers themselves understood this language literally.)

To speak of God intervening is misleading. In human life people only intervene from outside a situation; that is what the word means. But John invites us to see that the world, despite itself and unbeknown to itself, is always in God. That is its truth, and to come to the light is to recognize that this is the world's reality: it is from God, through God and in God, and cannot be otherwise. That is why, as this Gospel insists, to deny this reality is so destructive and death-dealing.

---

13 Nicholas Lash, *Seeing in the Dark: University Sermons*, London: Darton, Longman and Todd, 2005, pp. 59–64.

Will there be an end to the world?

It would be more faithful to the Bible to ask whether creation will be fulfilled, whether God will keep his covenant and complete his creative purpose. Scripture is unanimous in its positive answers to those questions, varied though they are.[14] And John's distinctive answer is to visualize this fulfilment, when the world itself comes to belief and to the knowledge of God (17.21, 23) in trinitarian terms.

A remarkable Christian of the twentieth century has expressed this well. Bede Griffiths spent 20 years as a monk in Britain before spending the second half of his long life in India. There he lived in an ashram, seeking to integrate Hindu and Christian liturgy, tradition and custom. A book published in 1989 was one product of this personal pilgrimage. Its title, *A New Vision of Reality: Western Science, Eastern Mysticism and Christian Faith*, and some of its language, takes us in the direction of John's Gospel. This is how he expresses the Christian view of the universe:

> Everything that returns to the Father returns through the Son and the Spirit, and so comes back transformed. This is the whole rhythm of the universe. It comes out through the Word into time and space. The Word is the . . . mind which organizes the universe, and the Spirit is the energy which develops the universe.[15]

Griffiths describes 'the rhythm of the universe' more fully in trinitarian terms: 'Everything comes forth from the Father, the Ground of Being, in the Son, the Word and Wisdom of the Father, and returns in the Spirit.'[16] We are 'only fulfilled when we are drawn back to our source . . . That is the ultimate meaning of the impulse of love.'[17]

---

14 This is not to overlook some of the New Testament's most negative images about the world's future in 2 Thessalonians, 2 Peter and Revelation. But even here the vision and hope of a 'new heaven' and a 'new earth' are retained (2 Peter 3.13; Revelation 21.1) and the image of fire in passages such as these should surely be understood metaphorically rather than literally.

15 Bede Griffiths, *A New Vision of Reality: Western Science, Eastern Mysticism and Christian Faith*, London: Collins, 1989, p. 171.

16 Griffiths, *A New Vision*, p. 251.

17 Griffiths, *A New Vision*, p. 172.

This is the vision of John for the world. The evangelist lived in tumultuous times, as we do. Our century will be, and already is, fertile soil for apocalyptic, both Christian and sub-Christian. Apocalyptic language and visions, like those in Revelation, come into their own in times of crisis, when the very foundations of our worlds or the world as a whole are threatened. But alongside apocalyptic language we also need this Gospel's vision of a world finally brought to the light through the 'lifting up' of One Crucified:

'And when I am lifted up from the earth I shall draw everyone to myself.' (12.32)

Conclusion

Readers may feel that the title of this chapter claims too much: no one can express the message of John's Gospel for today in just a few pages. There is always the risk of misreading and misunderstanding, anyway. But if these brief reflections prompt further study of John's Gospel in the light of the challenges which face both the Church and the world at large, they will have served their purpose.

John's Gospel carries on where the others leave off, developing more fully what is sometimes only implicit or less developed in them. The writer stands back from the controversies of Jesus' ministry, reflects on the experiences of his own community, and gives us his searching critique of the religious and the worldly opposition to the light who comes to save. Christian readers of the Gospel should not, in the first place, direct these critiques at anyone but themselves: 'if the cap fits . . .' If we read the Gospel with that kind of humility and self-criticism, then we shall be more able to receive its Jesus-centred message: here is One who reveals the very character of the invisible God, and who offers to satisfy the world's deepest hunger and thirst.

The disciples of Jesus were called to carry on the mission he had inaugurated. From their true centre of life in the Spirit, Son and Father, the Church of Jesus shares in God's mission to the world, its hallmark the selfless unity of the divine glory.

Suggestions for Further Reading

Commentaries on John's Gospel

R. A. Culpepper, *The Gospel and Letters of John*, Nashville: Abingdon, 1998.

K. Grayston, *The Gospel of John*, London: Epworth, 1990.

Andrew T. Lincoln, *The Gospel According to St John*, London: Continuum, 2005.

Also recommended

R. Edwards, *Discovering John*, London: SPCK, 2003.

C .R. Koester, *Symbolism in the Fourth Gospel*, Minneapolis: Fortress, 2003.

A Note for Discussion Groups

The book has been written for the non-specialist reader, including study groups who may wish to use it as a textbook for their study of John's Gospel. It will be important, of course, that the book does not displace the Gospel as the group's primary focus. I hope the following suggestions may help to facilitate that aim:

1   Use Chapters 1 and 2 – either or both, depending on time available – as background reading.
2   If the group wishes to work through as much of the Gospel as possible, section by section, Chapter 4 will help them to do that.
3   If the group wishes to grapple with the Gospel's more controversial features, and/or its significance for today, then Chapter 3 or Chapter 5 should provide them with more than enough material.